INTROVERTS

How to Use Your Introverted Personality for
Dating and Romantic Success

(Have the Courage to Live the Life You've Always
Wanted)

Edwin Chong

Published by Harry Barnes

Edwin Chong

All Rights Reserved

Introverts: How to Use Your Introverted Personality for Dating and Romantic Success (Have the Courage to Live the Life You've Always Wanted)

ISBN 978-1-7778032-0-9

ISBN 978-1-7778032-0-9

Legal & Disclaimer

The information contained in this book is not designed to replace or take the place of any form of medicine or professional medical advice. The information in this book has been provided for educational and entertainment purposes only.

The information contained in this book has been compiled from sources deemed reliable, and it is accurate to the best of the Author's knowledge; however, the Author cannot guarantee its accuracy and validity and cannot be held liable for any errors or omissions. Changes are periodically made to this book. You must consult your doctor or get professional medical advice before using any of the suggested remedies, techniques, or information in this book.

Upon using the information contained in this book, you agree to hold harmless the Author from and against any damages, costs, and expenses, including any legal fees potentially resulting from the application of any of the information provided by this guide. This disclaimer applies to any damages or injury caused by the use and application, whether directly or indirectly, of any advice or information presented, whether for breach of contract, tort, negligence, personal injury, criminal intent, or under any other cause of action.

You agree to accept all risks of using the information presented inside this book. You need to consult a professional medical practitioner in order to ensure you are both able and healthy enough to participate in this program.

Table of Contents

Introduction

This book contains steps and strategies on how to leverage your strengths as an introvert while being able to improve upon the weaknesses and self-doubts that riddle you with fear, anxiety, and stress.

Introversion is a major personality trait recognized in various personality theories. People who have this personality are known as introverts, and they tend to focus more on internal moods, feelings, and thoughts, instead of searching for external stimulation. Introverts are typically more reserved, introspective and quiet.

Unlike extroverts who tend to gain more energy when they are in a social setting and when they interact with others, introverts tend to lose most of their energy when they are in a social situation. This is the main reason why they feel the need to recharge after attending a party or a social function.

Note, however, that there is much more to being an introvert than just staying quiet and spending time alone within the four walls of your room. In fact, some of the greatest writers, artists, and most successful people in history, are self-proclaimed introverts. If you are an introvert, then learning how to tap into your creativity and the brilliance of your mind is what it takes to achieve success.

Your mind is home to the most creative thoughts, and you can display these for the whole world to see by overcoming your social anxiety, radiating confidence (especially when you are in a social setting), and conquering your fears.

This book is meant to be a key, or a portal, if you will, that can be used to achieve those goals. This book holds vital information that will allow you to utilize the power of your unique personality and become the most successful person that you can be. You will be taught some of the most effective tips in overcoming your social anxiety, boosting your confidence and conquering your fears in this book!

Thanks again for downloading this powerful guide; I hope you enjoy it and the life changing process that begins today! Let's get started!

Chapter 1: I Am An Introvert

There's ying, there's yang. There's male, there's female. There are introverts, there are extroverts. Duality makes life beautiful. We can all agree and the inherent beauty of all nature. Duality makes it so. However, there can't be more of one than there is of other. This causes imbalance, and consequent decay or destruction.

I grew up with my grandmother in a small town as an only child. Other members of the family came by often and I got all the attention a kid could wish for. It was great stuff. Yet, despite this attention, ever since I can remember, I preferred solitude. Solitude was a liberating and relaxing place from which I could be myself and freely explore the things in life. People and friends were nice too. But there was nothing like solitude.

"Gerald, I remember you would sit there with your toys for hours. You didn't care for anything else when you were in your own world", my mom reminded in a recent conversation.

"I was actually worried. You wouldn't cry, even when you were hungry. I even thought about taking you to a child therapist", she added. "But your grandma wouldn't let me. She said I should be grateful that you don't cry. It's less of a hassle".

That was me.

Let me fast-forward some years later to my elementary school years. This is when I noticed I was a bit different from the rest. During this time I took a great interest in card games. I loved collecting them to the point that most of my days were spent thinking up strategies on how to outwit my future opponents. It was great. I had a friend called David, and I'd run down to his apartment every day after school, and we'd play on his staircase. Our games continued for hours. Sometimes we had homework to do. If that was the case, it was always easy for us to get it done. We sped past our work and went back to focus on what was important- our card game. In my little world, I was the kid who had the most fun.

In their little world, I wasn't.

You see, everyone else in class by now was getting heavily into sports or other physical activities. The girls began dressing up nicer and getting into girl things. In class, gossip began to spread about the popular kids. As all of this occurred, I sat in class aloof. I felt a complete disconnect with what everyone else was doing and thinking. David, unfortunately, wasn't in my class so I had to wait until the school day was over to meet the only person in my social circle I could connect with. Was there something wrong with me?

Let's fast forward to high school.

High school began and whatever distance I between me and the others in class seemed to increase. As I entered my first class I felt lost. Everyone seemed so different than me. They were outspoken and made jokes in class. They dressed well and were in tune with fashion standards (something completely alien to me at that time and probably still now). The boys had girlfriends and the girls had boyfriends. I only had... myself. I loved girls and always have, but they just seemed so out of reach for me because I was so out of tune with the things I knew girls liked. As you might've guessed, I was an easy target for bullying.

My self-esteem plundered. My lack of confidence led me to overeat and further distance myself from other people. I developed strong social anxiety. I wasn't like them, so why waste my time trying to join them? I could always find refuge in my solitude.

I carried this emotional baggage along with me to college. I decided that was enough and decided to change who I was and become an 'extrovert'. I started reading self-help books and surrounding myself with people with social confidence, among many other things. I will be honest with you. I was able to eliminate the social anxiety that had begun to develop throughout late elementary school and high school. However, at the core, I was always an introvert.

While I did have success in social circles and achieved fluidity in working with others, it wasn't my natural state to be socially outgoing. I always had to put in an extra effort. It was then that I did something terribly wrong.

I wanted to prove myself that I too could be confident and assertive so badly that I began to identify only with my 'extroverted' self and dismiss my introverted qualities completely.

What ended up happening is that I lost touch with who I was at the core. Every time I came out of my house, I put on a persona that was radically different from who I was. I pushed myself to become ever more extroverted. As I did this, my anxiety began to resurface. I felt the need to be something different at every second of my life. It was too exhausting. What was I doing wrong?

I turned to books and experts for more answers. I realized two things: I wasn't accepting myself and I wasn't making use of my personal abilities and potential. It was like trying to teach a dog to meow. A dog certainly can meow (there's evidence of this on YouTube if you don't believe me), but are we making the best use of the animal's potential? I think not.

I am an introvert. I had to accept this. And from this place of authenticity, I had to discover the innate talents that come along with being an introvert.

And guess what?

I made a great discovery. There is a boundless power of learning, connection, leadership and introspection behind every introvert. I truly believe that if we, as introverts, truly understood the capacity and potential we have as human beings, we would not feel left out at all. There is a tremendous power within each one of us so let's not permit society to tell us otherwise.

Defining Introvert

To fully grasp the situation we're finding ourselves as introverts, we must define what an introvert is. According to Carl Jung, an introvert is simply somebody that gets their energy from within.

Where do you put your attention and get your energy?

Growing up, I spent most of my time in my own mind. It was time devoted to fantasizing about possibilities, growth and thriving. Sometimes I preferred dreaming an idea than actually living it. In my dreams, things always went my way. I felt comfort and power. As I grew older, I learned about the power of thoughts through self-help books and coaching. In the back of my mind, I already knew all of this. I had been living a world full of thoughts and dreams for as long as I can remember, and they had directed my every action.

Does this relate to you?

I want you to think about your own life. Throughout the day, where do you spend most of your time and where do you feel the best? Is it within or without?

Where do you find your place of power?

In The Social Anxiety Cure I explained that despite the fact that I am introverted, I have developed a lot of social skills. Today, when I know I'm about to come out of my 'inner world' and start talking and socializing with individuals either at work or business, I have rituals to get me going. I proactively do things to get myself off of my head and be able to flow in social settings. It's not a natural thing. People sometimes laugh in disbelief when I tell them I'm an introvert. If you meet me in a social setting, I don't seem like one. But behind the laughter and 'flow' I can pull off in social interactions, there's an introvert who'd much rather stay home and read a book.

I'm describing my situation because I want you to be able to identify where you fit into this. For some people, realizing they are introverted is pretty straightforward. Take Paul, he goes home, reads for hours and prefers spending time on his computer. Paul has a few friends but he treasures them greatly. Yup, that's pretty much an introvert- no doubt.

What about Susan though? She's always been pretty smart, even from a young age. Straight As were always her thing. Throughout high School and college, she saw her friends focusing more and more on parties and going to festivals. She did the same. Susan really wasn't herself in these situations, but she adapted and wound up developing a vibrant social life. In spite of this, sometimes she would really just prefer to stay home and read. She treasured the moments where she could be in solitude and spend time in the park or in nature. Would it be accurate to call her an introvert? Most of her friends would disagree. Her behavior doesn't really fit into the introvert stereotype of shyness and awkwardness society has sold us. But she is. And, perhaps, she hasn't even noticed herself that she is one.

If you've always thought yourself an extrovert and picked up this book by sheer curiosity, then I invite you to consider the possibility that you may be an introvert. Because of the preferences society has, many introverts have felt the need to develop their extroverted side and label themselves as extroverts. This is because of the social stigma placed on the word 'introvert'. This word might even conjure up adjectives such as awkward, socially inept, or submissive in your head. However, this couldn't be further from the truth.

Introvert Limitations and Other Myths

An introvert is not necessarily shy.

What?

I know. It's surprising.

Shyness is social anxiety. Social anxiety is a phobia, or as Thomas Richards, Ph.D., puts it, "the fear of being judged and evaluated negatively by other people, leading to feelings of inadequacy, inferiority, embarrassment, humiliation, and depression." Shyness, like any other phobia, arises out of past conditions where a person has associated negative feelings to social environments. It is this shyness that I help my readers eliminate through The Social Anxiety Cure. What I am not doing, however, is trying to change people into extroverts. That's not possible. Shyness is a fear and introversion is where you get power from. They're not related at all. You can be naturally extroverted and have social anxiety. To prove, I want you to think of a loud friend who won't stop talking but is unusually quiet when they meet somebody new. They almost seem… shy. That's probably because they are. Once they get past this initial shyness, they go back to being their loud and extroverted self.

It Just So Happens that Those Most Likely to Have Social Anxiety are Introverts (For Obvious Reasons).

Lacking a tendency and natural ability to develop strong social skills makes introverts prone to teasing and bullying. This raises the likelihood of introverts connecting fear with social settings. I know for a fact that I'm one of these cases.

Mike was one of the popular kids in my elementary school. I hated him. I didn't care about his popularity or my lack thereof. The real reason for my dislike was my infatuation with Chrystal. She was a lovely girl who was crazy about Mike and chose to stay with him even though he treated her badly (And yes, we're still talking about elementary school).

One day, as we were shifting around getting for a baseball game, Mike brushed past me. His shoulder collided with mine and pushed me back.

"Watch where you're going, idiot!" yelled Mike.

Everyone looked at me and I got very nervous. I sheepishly lowered my head and thoughts began racing in it. I didn't want to seem like a loser. "You're a jerk, Mike!" I yelled back. "You suck!"

Everyone around us laughed.

Mike threw his glove and speared towards me. We were face to face and his frame towered over me. I didn't plan to fight (nor did I know how), but I was determined to stick with what I said.

"Say that again", he dared me.

With my head kept down, I replied, "You suck man. Go die."

I felt a strong blow against my stomach that left me on the ground gasping for air. I felt a couple of kicks to my head and to my back. All I could think about was air; I couldn't breathe. Tears began to run down my cheeks.

The kids around me assumed different reactions. Some laughed and others felt compassion. The latter came to help me up after the beating I had received. The game ended abruptly and I decided to go home. I felt outright humiliated.

Sure, I was introverted as a kid; but I didn't have any fear of social interactions. I could approach people and make friends easily. That I chose not to engage with them so much, and spend my time playing cards or reading is a different story. However, from that day on, things changed. I was less prone to speak out and whenever there were a lot of people around, I would choose to leave. I didn't want to be publicly humiliated for the things I could say or do. The seed for fear of public embarrassment was planted in my heart and in my mind.

Unfortunately, many shy introverts share a similar story.

Introverts Love People Too

I can sum up this point with an activity I thoroughly enjoy: having a long conversation with a good friend over a bottle of wine (though beer works too).

Sure, you could always go to a party and drink your night away with a lot of people. But as an introvert, that doesn't appeal as much to me. More than likely, it is a draining experience to attend a party. For me, creating connection and meaning from a deep one on one conversation is much more alluring than partying with a lot of people. I'm sure other introverts can agree.

That being said, introverts love people; just like anybody else. However, we love building profound connections with few people. There's a preference in quality over quantity in this respect. We appreciate the wealth of thoughts, perspectives, and ideas within ourselves. This is why we seek to grasp the same inner wealth in others.

When I get to my desk and I start typing, I prefer people to be several feet away from me. Spaces I separate throughout the day for writing, reading, and exercise are something of a ritual for me. I don't need additional stimulation. I'd rather just get my activities done with.

However, I've grown accustomed to being seen as the angry loner by family when they come over and expect me to serve them and pamper them as an extrovert would.

I've caught my aunt sharing her insights about my behavior in more than one occasion during her visits. She would say something along the lines "Oh well, what else could you expect? He's so introverted."

In my mind, I'm thinking, "I'm not being a good host because I have priorities to tend to. Just like any other human being. Unfortunately, you're not one of them right now".

Some Introverts Love Being on Stage or Like to Perform

Let me share the story of Sebastian as an example. He loves speaking in public and he's great at it as well. He's someone whom I have built a very close connection to over the years. He's optimistic, determined and ready to do great things. I love that about him. Another thing I love is his talent for public speaking. I've been to several of his talks and he never ceases to amaze. When he is onstage, Sebastian can get you literally from cracking up to crying within minutes. His tone, timbre, spacing and overall delivery are always on point. It's incredible. Usually, after his talks, the audience goes to back to round him up for questions. It is in getting a close up that people realize that he's actually very calm and timid when speaking one on one.

I'm a good friend of Sebastian's and I can tell how different he is onstage from his everyday persona. As you get to know him, you realize he is highly intuitive and cares a lot for every person that he meets. He loves connecting with others deeply and is always careful when dealing with others' feelings. When he is alone, he does a lot of introspection to analyze the things in his life he's doing correctly and things he could improve on. There's a lot of inner work going there. It makes sense that his outward, social persona is almost too perfect. This is because, inwardly, he has worked hundreds if not thousands of hours to develop his extroverted qualities.

Guess what?

He's an introvert and he will tell you so himself. Nothing will change that.

And this leads to the next topic.

If You Take This Self-Help Course You Can Become an Extrovert... NOT

I write a lot about developing social skills and confidence. This might lead people to believe that I'm promoting extroversion; or that I'm trying to make people into extroverts. Far from it.

Let me sum it up with one idea: once an introvert, always an introvert.

Why?

Let's start with the biological, scientific reasons. Here are five:

Studies made by American psychologist Jerome Kagan proved how being introverted or extroverted was defined at birth and remained until death. This study was performed on groups of babies who were exposed to stimuli. Those with an over-reacting amygdala had a tendency to be more affected by the stimuli than those with a normal amygdala. One of the main factors that lead to introversion is an individual's ability to cope with social stimuli. Those with a sensitive amygdala will have a tendency to dislike social settings as a result.

Dr. Martin Olsen Laney writes in her book The Introvert Advantage: How to Thrive in an Extrovert World that introverts and extroverts process dopamine in very different ways. Dopamine is a substance segregated by your body that 'rewards' you. It's the great feeling you get from engaging in stimulating activities such as exercising, getting things done, facing fears, etc. You see, introverts are much more sensitive to dopamine than extroverts. Therefore, when dopamine races through the body of an introvert, they feel over-stimulated and anxious. Extroverts are less sensitive to it, and consequently, need more of it to get stimulated. As a result, they will pursue more action in order to get the amount of dopamine they need.

Our human nervous system is composed of two opposite sides: the sympathetic side and the parasympathetic side. I'll let you guess which of the two Introverts have a biological inclination towards. But before that, let's quickly go over the two. Let's start with the sympathetic side. It's the side responsible for the fight or flight response; which basically puts your body into overdrive: alertness rises, adrenaline is released, and muscles tense up. The parasympathetic side is responsible for the 'rest-digest' activities of your body. This allows your body to recuperate, store energy and provide maintenance to your body.

Have you already guessed? Yup, it's the parasympathetic.

Introverts use a longer thought process. Did you know that all the information we process goes through a pathway in our brains? The acetylcholine pathway is responsible for directing information and stimuli to different parts of our brains for processing. In the case of introverts, this pathway is much longer and travels to more places. Let me illustrate: When extroverts engage in the conversation, the information retrieved is sent for processing to areas in our brain where we process taste, touch, sight, and sound. It's a short path with a few stops. For introverts, however, information travels to all of those places and the right front insular (where empathy, reflection, and emotional meaning is processed), Broca's area (where speech is planned and where we activate in self-talk), the right and left front lobes (where we select, plan, and choose ideas or actions while developing expectations and evaluating outcomes), and the left hippocampus (which stores long-term memories). Introversion has much more to do with our brain chemistry and neural networks than we think. A casual interaction for an extrovert may be effortless; but for the introvert, it implies much more work.

The Journal of Neuroscience has published a study which found that introverts had more grey matter in their brain. Grey matter and the quantity of it in one's brain is an indicator of capacity for abstract thought and imagination. Extroverts, on the other hand, have been found to possess grey matter in smaller quantities, making them less apt for abstract thought. The more being researched on the topic, the more people realize how introversion is a quality that is innate to one's psyche. It's part of your individuality as a human being; It is part of what makes you you.

My friend, if you're an introvert, it's largely because you were born that way. Now the question is:

Would You Really Want It Any Other Way? Think about this.

I can make several parallels to make this point, but I think the following will be the most effective:

If you have an innate preference for a certain sex, would you really want to have it otherwise? If you're a gay female and you like women, nothing should change that; especially not society's expectations. The same goes if you're straight. Sure, curiosity or need may push introverts to develop extrovert skills. It's great to learn new things, and introverts can adapt and develop extrovert qualities. But at the end of the day, they will still be introverts.

Accepting and Thriving

The root problem of trying to become someone we're not is a lack of self-acceptance. This is why personal development is fundamental to our holistic growth as humans. Personal development begins first with self-acceptance and is then focused on bringing out your best self. The first step in regaining our personal power is owning up to our introversion.

A trait all human beings share is the desire to strive for more; a desire to be in constant growth. Maslow proves his Hierarchy of Needs. Self-actualization (a.k.a. achieving one's full potential, engaging in creative activities, and finding meaning and purpose) is the one human need that differentiates us from all the other animals in the animal kingdom. It's the highest of human needs that can only be met after one has covered his basic physiological and psychological needs. Sadly, most people spend their time only trying to meet their most basic needs.

In nature, that which does not grow is dying. We must keep growing only to stay alive. And by 'alive', I don't mean just having a heartbeat. I mean living life to the fullest extent and thriving every single conscious moment. I agree with Helen Keller that, "Life is either a daring adventure or nothing at all."

This is the premise behind my work. This book is an invitation to find yourself as an introvert and to make use of the power resides within you to enrich your life.

There is greatness that can be achieved if people were to turn inward to face their problems. Now, more than ever, people are disconnected to this power. The long work hours and constant cell phone notifications keep us from going within. But, as introverts, we have an advantage over the rest that our inner world is where we spent most of our time. Let's make full use of it

Chapter 2: Personality Types And How To Motivate Them To Get Their Best Supports

Did you know that some horses will follow you for a carrot, while other horses won't budge unless you whack them with a stick? Well, people are also motivated by either carrots, or sticks. Some people move towards goals. Other people move away from consequences.

As earlier mentioned, psychologists have identified four distinct personality types: Sanguine, Phlegmatic, Melancholic and Choleric. Everyone leans towards one of these types. If you learn to understand what excites, motivates, irritates and frustrates these different personality types, you'll be well on your way to understanding why certain people frustrate you more than others.

Sanguine and Choleric personalities tend to be fast-paced and impulsive. If you dangle a carrot in front of them, they'll probably jump at the carrot. On the other hand, Phlegmatic and Melancholic personalities tend to be slower-paced and indecisive. To get them into gear, you sometimes have to show them the sticky consequences of not taking a risk.

"Carrot" people go to the dentist because they want white teeth. "Stick" people go to the dentist because they don't want cavities. "Carrot" people try new things because they want to get ahead and be in the know. "Stick" people try new things because they don't want to fall behind, or mess things up.

Can you see the difference?

Here's another personality trait that you should consider. Melancholic and Choleric personalities tend to be internally validated. In other words, they carry inside themselves a strong sense of their own opinions and their own sense of right. If you give Cholerics too much feedback, they'll ask you to mind your own business.

If you give Melancholics illogical feedback, they'll throw their hands up in frustration.

In contrast, Sanguine and Phlegmatic personalities tend to be externally validated. Meaning, they need people to validate them, and they only thrive when others support them. In fact, they often value your opinion more than they value their own. If you don't give a Sanguine enough feedback, you'll likely be tracked down and asked what you think; while Phlegmatics can't make a decision without considering how everyone around them is affected by the decision.

Basically, Melancholic and Choleric personalities tend to make decisions based upon what they think, want, or need; while Phlegmatic and Sanguine personalities tend to make decisions based upon what others think, want, or need. That being the case, whenever you want to present a solution, opinion, or idea to someone, you should probably consider that person's personality type because unless your solution motivates his or her type, you're wasting your time and confusing the issue.

Whatever personality type you're dealing with, you make your most effective and persuasive presentations when you show each type how they can get what they want by agreeing to work with you...

Chapter 3: How To Deal With Introverts?

 "Every time we stomp down our introverted nature, we crush part of our soul in the process." ~ Michaela Chung

So, now there is a question that the world needs an

answer, why are we making introverts feel guilty? People used to value man of action over man of words and plans. Introverts have fears that not all can understand, only introverts know what they feel when they hear a doorbell or a knock at the door, they are even petrified when they hear their phone ringing. Some introverts love doing their laundry, it's like bathing your kids without having to speak to them. Introverts hate fighting, and shouting, you will barely see them indulging into a fight; another thing that irritates introverts is random sounds like ticking of a clock at midnight, screeching of a chalk on a board or a squeaking chair. Some introverts get intimidated easily, it may be due to lack of confidence and selfworth, or maybe due to lesser experience with human interactions, which may cause shaking out of nervousness and even panic or anxiety attacks as well. Introverts avoid social situations, and they love to crash on the bed after school, office or any social meeting. Introverts like spending weekends in the bed unlike other people who are busy partying at night clubs.

I actually had an argument with my friends for not being able to go to night club, that is something which I don't even want to try because I know even a few moments spent over there will drain away all my energy and that will spoil my weekend along with theirs. I am fortunate enough to get friends who understand me and respect my choices. I find it really hard getting closer to people, however once I start trusting someone, I trust them blindly. Some of the activities that I feel are fun for us (introverts) scrolling down the social media with no specific purpose, smiling inside our minds and hitting the like buttons unnecessarily; clicking selfies rather asking others to click a picture. Being alone feels so good to an introvert, they will only talk to someone if they are better than their solitude. Other fun things include being with nature rather than being with people. An introvert packs for a picnic by putting a camera and a book (and maybe a diary) in their bag pack, all set to write or to read a book.

Introverts are happy to be alone. Some of us may be socially awkward, however most of us know how to socialize with people and be the life of the party. They choose to be alone and avoid interactions, try to understand them much better and share with the world, whatever you learn about them. Let the world clear their vision tainted by prejudice. Introverts have only a handful of expectations and need, like they want you to text them and not call. I want the people to change the way theylook at introverts, don't think of introversion as something that needs to be cured; spend your free time the way you like, not the way you think you are supposed to. Everyone should have a right to live the way they want and a right to do whatever they want in their free time without anyone judging and commenting on what they should be doing.

When introverts say they are busy, or they have plans with others, it might not always be the truth, they fear that you may not understand about how someone can have plans with themselves, so introverts say that they have plans elsewhere or with others. Most people misunderstand introverts; introverts don't hate people; they just need more time alone to recharge their energy. Furthermore, introverts can articulate their thoughts clearer in writing than while speaking. When they aren't talking, they are just listening or perhaps day-dreaming. It is a fact that seldom are they actually in a bad mood. People label introverts as people who are shy, book nerd, too serious or someone who hates people. In writing introverts can express their thoughts easily, however verbally, it is not that easy. They plan their weekends in a different way than most of the people, it's their duty to respect and follow their social calendar, so they plan their time to hang out with friends and then time to recover from hanging out with friends.

Nowadays it's a little bit different everyone has to prove themselves in the town of strangers, in terms of social skills. Now people are concerned about their names, their social status and being tagged as an "influencer", that's how our society is, we are living in today.

To me, social skills are unimportant the thing that matters is how much you know and   how knowledgeable are you about something. It's more important to know when to speak than to know what to speak. There are armies of people coming together to "improve" introverts and suggest things to help them be extroverts. Let them be themselves so that they can come with the solutions with best of their capability. People who are modest and introvert, can take a day off just because they did not want to see or talk to people. Some have issues eye contacting; they want to be alone or be with someone else who wants to be alone. Introverts at times, end the conversation prematurely for the fear that I might drain my energy and too much of your time. I like spending time alone in the library, I am rarely bored alone; I am often bored in groups and crowds.

My journey to become an ambivert involved a lot of efforts and practicing stuff that I never had tried in the past; like public speaking and self-motivation to talk with people and small talks. I tried to learn, read, write, think and research about how to talk to people and how to deal with social interactions. Trust me it was really hard because this is not my natural thing. Only an introvert knows what they have to deal with while talking with people. I want people to stop the madness for group work, they must understand that individuals can too perform equally well too. Introverts crave meaning in everything so party chitchat feels like sandpaper to our brain. They need much more privacy; more autonomy and we need to teach them to work on their own and not to depend on the team. An introvert may feel asocial when pressured to go to a party that doesn't interest them. Because for them, such events do not promise meaningful interaction. In fact, they know that the party will leave them feeling more alone and alienatedso they feel it's better to avoid such functions.

People think they know us; but we are 90 per cent hidden under the ocean. I believe the real me is a little bit different, I behave differently with different people, I have altogether a different personality with my friends versus the people who are not close to me. There is a huge gap in things that others think we do, versus what we actually do and what we think of doing. We wait for payday and do nothing when the salary hits our account. We need to tell our introverts friends to calm down and not to push themselves till they have a mental breakdown.

When someone talks continuously it depletes our energy, we usually take a deep breath and quietly sit in a chair with headphones on our ears even if no song is playing. I personally avoid exchanging gifts because it drains a lot of energy, asking someone what they like, choosing something for them, thinking about it if they will like it or not. It's too much of a potential conversation. So, I avoid taking gifts and giving it to someone.I couldn't really communicate this to my friends fearing, they will not understand.

If I like something, I keep it to myself I won't necessarily appreciate it and talk about that. It's just I want to conserve as much energy as I can. I am not really comfortable with talking to people who speak closely to my face. I like to keep distance and I want you to respect me for what I am and what I like or dislike. I am too sensitive to touch, I continuously think about it and it drains my energy, even if someone's knee is touching my bag. I would like to sit separate from everyone in a bus than sitting next to someone. In my school, I was the quietest kid in the room. We are not anti-social; we just have a different way to socialize. All the introverts have an adventure land inside of their own mind. I would like to convey a message to all my friends who consider themselves as introverts to go in the wilderness and build their own revelations; unplug and get inside their head a little more often, explore their mind and give themselves some time to introspect and discover a little more frequently.

People think that I am shy when they first meet me, but I am not shy, I am just not really interested in some randomtopic, that's why I don't feel an urge to add something invaluable to it. We have already established about how bad the weather outside is today and about how sad we are for the team that lost the match last week and I nodded my head. I being an introvert am energy efficient; by nodding my head I was participating in the conversation which implies that you can consider my nod as a response, so why do I have to waste my energy to speak up.

Chapter 4: Being An Introvert Doesn't Mean You Have Insecurity— Here's Why

Another misconception about introverts is that they are insecure people. This is wrong. People should not generalize because it's a fact that even some extroverts are insecure and some of them are shy, too.

Some people are mainly anti-social or have low self-esteem. Does this mean that they are introverted? No. As you can recall, the given characteristics of introverts does not include not being self-confident or being very self-conscious. You have to come to terms with the fact that introverts mostly just choose the way they want to live instead of just following what others are doing. This means that they have more self-confidence than others because they are sure of themselves and they do not feel the need to fit in. If you think about it, those who think that it's important to do what others are doing just for the heck of it are those that should be considered insecure instead of those who go through life on their own terms.

When someone becomes reclusive or when he shies away from society because of his own inhibitions and fears, he is often thought of as one who is introverted. Again, you have to realize that everyone has their own set of fears and limitations; everyone has something that makes them feel bad about themselves. Some people have to seek the help of professionals such as psychiatrists to help them with their condition. There is nothing wrong with this just as there's nothing wrong with being an introvert.

Introverts are powerful because they can stand on their own two feet and they don't need the approval of the world just so they could feel good about themselves—that makes them some of the most confident people in the world.

Chapter 5: Perceptions Of Introverts

Introverts are widely misperceived by the world as holding back from participating in society, when in fact, they just prefer to function in a different way. This chapter aims to debunk common myths regarding introverts and set the record straight about what actually makes and introvert an introvert.

Myths About Introverts

Introverts Are Withdrawn: It's easy to see why this myth has often been interpreted as fact. While it may sometimes seem that introverts dislike participating, the truth of this myth is that many introverts simply prefer to spend time alone. Many introverts cite needing to be alone in order to recharge and gain energy, as opposed to extroverts who need other people to gain energy. When an introvert turns down an invitation to attend a party, it is often not for personal reasons and is actually due to a simple need for alone time.

Introverts Never Say Anything: This actually could not be farther from the truth. Rather than sharing an excess amount of information, introverts would rather only speak up when their words will add depth to the conversation. If they are in a small group and the topic holds particular interest to the introvert, they will be more than happy to contribute to the conversation.

Introverts Don't Fit In: This myth has solid foundations for a simple reason: the modern America caters specifically to extroverts. It's an extremely unfortunate and unfair bias, and while it does not stop introverts from doing well, it does make it harder. Susan Cain, author of Quiet: The Power of Introverts in a World That Can't Stop Talking, has noted that American classrooms and workplaces have been designed to cater to extroverts. She notes that classroom desks used to be arranged in rows and work was largely completed independently. Now, however, students sit in pods and work both in the classroom and in the workforce is often done in groups, further isolating introverts and forcing them to work in environments that are over stimulating. While active stimulation does help extroverts to get their brains going, introverts require a quieter workspace. Thus, it's not that introverts don't fit in, but rather that the most common spaces in American society are not always constructed to accommodate the needs of all its inhabitants in an unbiased fashion.

Shyness and Introversion is the Same Thing: This is another point that Susan Cain addresses in her Ted Talks episode, The Power of Introverts. Cain defines shyness as "fear of social judgment," whereas introversion is "more about how you respond to stimulation, including social stimulation." Webster-Merriam Medical Dictionary offers as a similar definition, stating that introversion is "the act of directing one's attention toward or getting gratification from one's own interests, thoughts, and feelings." Thus the reasoning behind an introvert not interacting in the same way as an extrovert is not due to shyness, but is merely due to a different source of inspiration. In short, extroverts look outside of themselves for stimulation and introverts refer to their own imaginations.

Introverts Never Have Any Fun: Here is a myth completely perpetuated by extroverts who have extreme difficulty relating to an introvert's style of living. The truth of the matter is, introverts like to have fun; they just don't want to experience it in the same manner as extroverts. For most introverts, the thought of going to a crowded bar to meet new people is not fun, it's nerve-wracking. A night at home with a bottle of wine and one friend may sound much more appealing than a bar and reap the same benefits of socialization. Additionally, introverts tend to be extremely observant and absorb information more quickly than extroverts, making crowded outings exhausting. It's no surprise then that they prefer alternate means of entertainment, and if it works for them, then why shouldn't they?

Introverts Can Become Extroverts: While many have tried, introverts cannot magically turn themselves into extroverts. Being an introvert is an essential part of the personality and even effect brain patterns. However, introverts can practice social skills and with time be able to function similar to an extrovert during large group socialization, though the extroverted behavior will never truly be a natural part of their thought process. The same is true for extroverts: a true extrovert will grow bored and wither if they stay in their apartment all weekend. Ask an introvert to do the same thing and they will probably show up Monday morning with a self-penned book in hand.

Introvert Personality Traits/Types

Introverts are often lumped together and thought to have all of the same introverted characteristics and personality traits. And while many introverts can argue differently, there is now scientific proof that debunks the myth. In 2015, New York Magazine published an article by Melissa Dahl detailing the findings of psychologist Jonathan Cheek, who noted that the experiences voiced by many self-described introverts were significantly different than established medical definitions. Curious as to what the discrepancy was, Cheek conducted a study in which he spoke with numerous self-proclaimed introverts alongside his graduate students and found that there are actually four different types of introversion: social, thinking, restrained, and anxious. A single individual may have only one or even every type of introversion as a part of their personality. Cheek further conducted his study by measuring individuals' varying degrees of introversion. For example, an individual may be 40% socially introverted, 20% thinking, 70% restrained, and only 10% anxious. While Cheek admits that his questionnaire to determine these factors is mostly a working model, his inquisitive examination of the term introversion is one that has been met with relief and praise from frequently misunderstood introverts. This comes as no surprise since, according to Susan Cain; a third to one half of the population is introverted. With such an enormous portion of the human race declaring themselves as such, even if it is just to themselves, it is validating to see research results that shed some light on the introvert as an individual. Below are the four types of introversion as categorized by Cheek.

Social: This type of introversion has been referred to most often in this book and is often people's first thought association when asked about introversion. Essentially, those who are socially introverted would either be with only a few people or alone rather than interact in large groups. Of course, as demonstrated by Cheek's questionnaire, an individual may experience this to different degrees. If the individual scores 100% socially introverted on Cheek's scale, they will rarely ever interact with others. However, someone who scores 40% may enjoy large group interaction in small doses and then need to be alone for a while afterwards to recharge and process all of the recently absorbed stimuli.

Restrained: Here is a type of introversion that greatly benefits workers. Restrained introversion depicts those who prefer to gather their thoughts before they speak and are usually a little lost among the fast paced conversational style of more extroverted individuals. However, this characteristic also causes individuals to be highly cautious, express decidedly formulated thoughts, and make well-informed decisions, which is partly what makes them such excellent candidates for leadership positions.

Anxious: This form of introversion can be mostly closely associated with shyness, although it has different characteristics. Shyness and anxious introversion both cause the individual to feel awkward in social situations, making networking and forming new friendships with strangers into an intensely uncomfortable experience. However, where shyness will fade once the individual has escaped from the situation, anxious introversion may persist. That is not to say anxious introversion is a fleeting type of introversion; it is a core part of an individual's personality. Thus, it makes those who have this particular characteristic tend to be intensely reflective and often contemplate stressful matters obsessively, leaving them exhausted and with a semi-constant sense of pervading anxiousness.

Thinking: Those who adhere to thinking introversion are often highly created and have rich inner lives. This is because thinking introversion involves intense self-reflection and often manifests itself in a highly imaginative and thoughtful individual. While this type of introversion does not affect a person's ability to enjoy more populated social gatherings, it can cause the individual to grow distracted, much the same as how extroverts will grow bored when there is less stimuli.

Chapter 6: Unique Leadership Qualities Of Introverts

It's rare that you see the words "introvert" and "leader" in the same sentence. After all, the common perception is that extroverts make great public speakers and are excellent networkers -- two things CEOs and organizational leaders must be -- and that introverts are not. We often expect corporate executives to conform to certain extroverted CEO stereotypes: C for charismatic, E for effusive, and O for outgoing. In fact, a poll conducted by USA Today cited 65 percent of executives who believed introversion to be a barrier to leadership. I understand the insecurity that comes with being an introvert and a leader. The assumption that extroverts make better leaders has permeated our culture. However, there's a paradox at the heart of how we think about leaders. Ask someone to picture a stereotypical leader and most people will think of someone confident, brash, and outgoing--the classic extrovert. But ask a person to think of real-life business visionaries and many of the people they're likely to name, from Bill Gates to Warren Buffet, are textbook examples of introverts. It may not seem like it at first glance, but many introverted people can become better leaders than extroverted people, it just takes a lot more effort. Not only are introverted people usually better organized on average but, as mentioned before, they also have a greater capacity for strategizing, understanding and reading people, listening to stakeholders and assessing happenings in the environment. How do these introverted leaders do it? How do they thrive in the extroverted business world? They seek to understand—and play to—their strengths. Here are unique leadership skills that help introverted leaders build on their quiet strength and succeed -

Unique Leadership Skills

Introverts are prudent.

Unlike their extroverted counterparts who are more sensitive to rewards, which explain why extroverts are more pre-disposed to risk-taking, introverts take a circumspect approach to chance. This is why you hear extroverts say things such as, "Let's just do it!" whereas introverts prefer to ask, "are we sure this is the right thing to do?" Why is this an entrepreneurial advantage? Risk-taking is a rite of passage for any founder yet can often feel awkward. You may vacillate between yes and no, go and no-go while you weigh different options. Now you know why. Recognizing how you're predisposed to decision-making is how you improve, and entrepreneurs make impactful decisions every day. Second, while every startup necessitates some risk to propel it forward, it also requires prudence in capital and resources.

Introverts learn by listening.

Rather than the flashy chit-chat that defines social gatherings, introverts listen intently to what others say and internalize it before they speak. They're not thinking about what to say while the other person is still talking, but rather listening so they can learn what to say. They are intrinsically motivated and therefore seek content regardless of achieving an external standard. Quiet bosses with proactive teams can be highly successful, because introverted leaders carefully listen to what their followers have to say. Extroverted leaders, on the other hand, can be a liability if their followers are extroverts who like to take the initiative and make suggestions. This is because extroverted leaders are generally less receptive to proactivity: They end up doing a lot of the talking and not listening to any of the ideas that the followers are trying to provide. They're more effective with passive subordinates who are comfortable with being told what to do. Introverted leaders are more suited to carefully process and implement their team's ideas. Introverts leverage their quiet nature.

This is how introverts leverage their power of presence: they "own" the moment by speaking calmly and deliberately, which translates to a positive perception. One of the greatest advantages introverts have is their ability to stay focused, where others around them might be distracted. They're generally not afraid of solitude because they know it's fruitful. It gives them opportunities for self-reflection, thinking, theorizing, observing, planning or imagining, not to mention reading, researching and writing. Our culture discourages time alone, but in our noisy world, with its many distractions, we can get an edge if we carve out some time for solitude. It helps to minimize distractions and aids in staying more focused. It improves our ability to think. Introverts can teach us a lot in that regard.

Introverts demonstrate humility.

Not to say that extroverts aren't humble, but introverts tend to have an accurate sense of their abilities and achievements (not to be confused with underestimated). Humility entails the ability to acknowledge mistakes, imperfections, knowledge gaps and limitations -- all key ingredients for getting ahead in business and life. Being humble also indicates an openness to hear new ideas or receive contradictory information. Servant leadership is characterized by a primary desire to be of service to others and to empower followers to grow. Servant leaders believe their company goals are best achieved by developing the potential of their workers. They're not self-seeking and interested in grabbing the limelight. On the contrary, they want to shine the light on others in the pursuit of a greater purpose: the success of their organizations, projects or ventures. It takes humility to do this, but humility pays.

Introverts manage uncertainty.

Since introverts have a lower sensitivity to external rewards than extroverts, they're more comfortable working with little information and resisting self-defeating impulses. Introverts are also more likely to persist in finding solutions that aren't initially apparent. Don't believe me? Maybe you'll believe Albert Einstein, who said, "It's not that I'm so smart, it's that I stay with problems longer." Finding certainty where uncertainty typically prevails is a huge plus for any entrepreneur.

A calming demeanor is good for business.

Introverts are not only quieter than extroverts, but they're also generally calm and collected. In noisy and chaotic organizations, which are often cauldrons of emotion, an introvert's presence is like a salve to the psyche. Their quiet energy is a hidden asset. The introvert's even temper creates a peaceful atmosphere that engenders trust and safety for those around them. Trust, in turn, helps us do business more effectively. Staying stable and calm in all situations—cultivating equanimity and composure—are the hallmarks of introverts. These attitudes can radiate to others in the workplace, and especially to customers. We can all sense when we enter a business if employees are on edge, which has a detrimental effect on our customer relation experience. If the operative word is calm, the introverts can teach others a thing or two.

They don't settle.

Introverts aren't known for their self-satisfaction, this continual striving for improvement can be a huge benefit in business settings. Introverts are likely to be aware about areas where they need to improve. This type of focus and awareness is very important to the growth of a leader and their team. This will to challenge oneself will motivate teams to do the same by evaluating themselves, their colleagues, and the team to improve."

Think effective leadership requires gregariousness and charisma? Think again. Introverts actually can be better leaders than extraverts, especially when their employees are naturally proactive. The myth that introverts are less effective leaders than their extroverted brethren is just that. Leverage your personality strengths to lead your business no matter what side of the spectrum you fall on. While there are certainly pros to being an extrovert, an introvert's ability to defer to others, silently process information, and take a break from social interaction clearly has its benefits! If you're an introvert, don't disqualify yourself from leadership positions. Don't feel insecure in your position (or your call) as a leader. The world needs you.

Chapter 7: What Is Keeping You From Becoming Extroverted

You are actually responsible as to why you are so introverted. Stop saying that you are born the way you are right now, you can change yourself to become the kind of person you have always wanted to be. The reason why your introverted side has become so dominant is your way of thinking. To give you an idea on how you are keeping yourself from becoming more of an extrovert, here are the mental stumbling blocks mentioned in the previous chapter.

You undervalue extroversion

Since you are an introvert, you may think that you do not need to be around other people to live a life that you consider "normal". As said earlier, there is nothing wrong about spending time alone, but you should not discount the benefits that you can get when you socialise with other people. For instance, you will meet new friends, you will learn new things that will let you grow as a person, you will be able to laugh and enjoy yourself.

However, this does not mean you have to place less value on being an introvert; it is all about striking a balance between the two. You can still look forward to spending some time alone at home after a day of socialising with other people; you can use this "me time" to catch up on your reading, meditate, or watch an episode or two of your favourite TV show. Then after you had enough time to yourself, you just need to go out and socialise, rinse and repeat.

You hang out with the wrong kinds of people

Maybe the reason why you cannot seem to force yourself to socialise is because your current social circle is not really conducive to having fun. If you surround yourself with people who you do not really like then that may just be the reason why you are the way you are right now. If you think that being sociable means hanging out with the kind of people you would rather not be around with then finding the motivation to meet new people will be a bit hard.

It is about time you do something about your small social circle, go out and expand your network of friends and acquaintances. Do not think that you will not find people who you actually want to spend time with, they are out there, you just need to pull yourself up by the bootstraps and go find them.

You think socialising online is enough for you

In this day and age where social media is king, you may think that interacting with other people online fulfils your quota for "human" interaction, but sadly, it does not. Yes, the internet have made it easier for people to get in touch with each other; people can now chat with each other even when they are on opposite sides of the globe, and they can get a glimpse of what is happening in their lives thanks to social networks like Facebook and Twitter. However, virtual socialisation cannot hold a candle to face-to-face communication.

When you talk with another person face to face, you form a kind of emotional bond with each other. Not only does talking transmit information faster than typing it on a keyboard, you also receive the non-verbal cues. You will know that the other person feels strongly about his idea when you sense the excitement in his/her voice while speaking, and on the other hand, you will know if he/she is opposed to your opinion when he/she uses a defensive tone of voice. You might think that you can get all these through video chats, but that tone of voice is not the only non-verbal cues that people use. People also touch each other to stress their points or to make other people understand that they are on the same side.

You do not have any social skills whatsoever

Is the reason why you do not like to attend parties is because you have absolutely no idea what you have to do when you get there. You do not have to worry too much about this because you can learn social skills. Sociable people were not born that way, their environment and upbringing moulded them into the kind of people they are now.

Even if you did start learning social skills a bit later in life, it does not mean you will not be able to gain them; yes, you can teach an old dog new tricks.

You think you will become the kind of extrovert that you hate

Yes, there are extroverts who are downright noisy and annoying, but it is wrong that you will become that kind of person. If you think you will only become the kind of person who would talk to someone at a party and then forget that person's name the morning after then you are wrong.

You can become the kind of extrovert that you have always wanted to be. You can choose to become not the obnoxious type, just someone who can comfortably start a conversation with a complete stranger, but still be genuinely interested in what the other person is saying. In other words, you can avoid being the kind of person who socialises just for the heck of it.

These are only some of the mental barriers that are preventing you from empowering your extroverted side. Search deep within yourself and find which one of these thoughts are hindering your personal growth. There is no point in denying having any of these limiting beliefs, you just need to accept them and then focus your energy to making sure that you no longer actively think about them anymore. Yes, it will take some time to get used to a new way of thinking, and it will definitely feel awkward at the start, just keep a stiff upper lip and move on.

Chapter 8: Developing A Healthy Self-Image

Introverts should also be mindful of their self-image. First, they should become aware of how their appearance affects the behavior of other people around them. People react different to you based on how you look. If you are not projecting a confident and engaging persona, others might be hesitant to start a conversation with your, or engage with you socially.

You can make it easier for people to accept you by improving your image. Your overall image includes the way you dress, the way you groom yourself and the way you body language - the way you carry yourself. You do not need to buy all the trendy clothes to be accepted by the people around you. All you need to do is to find a socially acceptable style of dressing that you are comfortable with and and that boosts your confidence.

While extroverts prefer to use their clothing to stand out, introverts do not have this weight on their shoulders. Introverts can practically wear anything they are comfortable with, and that helps them blend in with the crowd.

Your image should match your life goals

Your image is an important part of your success. You should design your image so that it aligns with what you are trying to achieve. Let's say you are an introvert and you have an idea for a business. You know that the odds of your business becoming a success are higher if you have a business partner. You start to look for people who are also interested in the type of business that you want to start.

You decided that you want to work with a millennial. The best way to convince a millennial to work with you is by showing them that you share their views. However, just telling them your vision will not be enough to convince them, you also need to look like a successful entrepreneur.

Control your online image

When designing your overall image, be mindful of how you present yourself online. When applying for your dream job for example, you should expect that the people in charge of checking your credentials would look you up online. If you want to have a better image, you should control all the things written about you online.

You can start with your social media accounts. You should clean up the image that you portray in these accounts. For instance, you should hide any pictures and videos that can negatively affect your professional image. You don't have to delete them permanently, they're still your memories after all, you just have to tweak a couple of settings so that only your closest friends have access to them.

Create a favorable reputation

Aside from controlling your online image, you should also be aware of your reputation among your colleagues, your friends and your family. You can shape your reputation through the actions that you show other people. You can start building your reputation through what you show online. However, you should back your online claims up with real life actions and results.

All your actions and decisions should lead to a good reputation. If you have a positive reputation, it will be easier for you to interact with the people who know who you are. People will treat you based on what they have heard about you.

Keep doing introvert activities you enjoy

Most introverts try to remove their natural tendencies when they learn to be more social. You should not completely remove these activities from your life. If you like spending time alone, you should do it. You should do what keeps you happy. Many of your introvert activities are part of your identity. You cannot just remove them from your schedule.

Chapter 9: Start With Yourself

People have experienced very unique ways to find themselves and their strengths. Due to life changing circumstances, some can go from one extreme personality type to another. This is why attaching yourself to the characteristics of introversion doesn't matter. You can possibly change overtime with self-refinement and new experiences. Your unique personality is created through culture, knowledge, genetics and the influence of life experiences.

Consider the neuroplasticity of the brain.

The brain has an amazing ability to reshape, evolve and develop depending on the state of its health. It changes through new experiences and other environmental factors. For example, gray matter develops in the brain as you learn a new language or skill. Any physical or emotional trauma, and changes in fitness and diet will also affect its state.

This also means that personality, mood, energy, confidence and fear perception can change. If you are motivated enough to improve those things, you can start by taking care of your brain chemistry through healthy changes in diet, fitness and proactive learning.

1) The first and most vital step you must take is to improve your overall health and fitness. By consuming a complete diet of whole foods and vital supplements, plus adequate physical activity, you can support the balance of your entire body and brain chemistry. Consume foods, herbs and supplements that provide the complete nutrients for what your body and mind need, and avoid anything that will cause inflammation and toxic effects.

When you balance your brain chemistry, you will accelerate your complex learning skills and have heightened cognitive comprehension. You will become more receptive to the positive changes in your life, as your mind will recognize even the subtle opportunities that can contribute to your growth and survival. You will also have better mood control, which strengthens your emotional threshold for life's challenges. Speak to a health professional, nutritionist and fitness trainer for a development program customized for you.

2) Consider therapy or medication if you believe that you may have the more severe traits of social anxiety. Please speak with a mental health professional for further guidance.

3) Evaluate your social environment. Pay attention to the social life and culture that you are constantly surrounded with. Think of the types of personalities that you are frequently exposed to. Acknowledge their attitudes, value systems, ambitions, intentions, motivations, consistent actions, communication styles, conflict management skills, initiatives and relationship qualities. You are the sum of the top 5 people who are constantly in

your life. Their personal qualities and level of emotional support transfer onto you very profoundly.

You must be around people who will be on the same journey as you, and are actively supportive of your goals. Seek out the people who have the qualities you want to emulate, especially the ones who are open to help and deeply understand you. Find mentors, support groups, forums, meet-ups, trainers, teachers or leaders... Being in the presence of people whose traits you'd like to adapt will truly affect you overtime.

4) Reduce unnecessary distractions from your life, especially your usual comfort mechanisms. A lot of people "escape" into entertainment media such as movies, video games, TV, radio and various leisure activities. You can unwind with these, but they cannot use up the majority of your days. What you do with your time alone will influence your approach to relationships. What entertainment

provides you with is a temporary sense of relief, but also a modification in your sense of reality and communication style, which will affect your practical interactions with the real world

The time you spend with people is more important than the time you spend with things. Complex social interactions may be more challenging and emotionally demanding than playing a fantasy video game, but with persistence, patience and consistent investment, you can make all of your relationships deeply rewarding for a lifetime.

5) Read constantly. Learn new perspectives about life. Develop opinions. The more you have **feelings and thoughts** about people and events, the more opportunity you have to express them. What you read and how much of it is highly important as well. We absorb our information through sources such as newspapers, magazines, leisure books, entertainment websites and comics. You

have to read what is immediately necessary to your goals, so you don't go through information overload. Be extremely selective of the quality of information, and the amount of information that you read.

Information overload will make you over think and stuck in your own head. You can get overwhelmed, confused, and incongruent. Simplify the kinds of information that enter your head and what shapes your opinion. Being well read is one way that you can have a conversation about **anything**.

To aid in your long-term learning efforts, you can boost your memory with the strategic combinations of brain-enhancing foods, supplements, herbs and nootropics (also called neuro-enhancers).

6) You can also improve your conversations by practicing mental presence. Being more in tune with yourself emotionally and having a higher self-awareness will allow you to have the

intuition and creativity to react in situations that are unique to you. The combination of meditation, reading and improved physical and mental health will raise your self-awareness and emotional presence. This internal balance will help you be present in the moment, more out of your head, and create good feelings from within during interactions. Even if you don't know what to say during a conversation, your good mood, energy and heightened mental awareness will boost the creativity to come up with anything randomly.

Varied social interactions also provide you with reference experiences for building relationships. The more you practice, the more you can create something profound from any type of conversation, even the ones that start off as surface level small talk. You can reflect on those references and define your own unique identity. Challenging life experiences strengthen your character, so never shy away from pushing your own comfort zone. Don't worry about embarrassing situations. We all started the same way. As you consistently meet new personalities, your confidence will develop and the way you handle newer situations will improve.

Also consider some improvisational comedy classes for a fun way of practicing your creativity and intuition. Improv will help you to focus, think creatively, and develop a quick wit in the present moment.

As you learn to harness the positive feelings and energy within yourself, you can transfer your state onto the people you interact with. As people respond to energy, they will reciprocate whatever you are outputting. Whatever you feel, they will feel.

7) Develop the habit of being proactive. Changing what you've been comfortable with requires a high level of motivation and genuine desire to change. Having the

support of a strong social circle will definitely help you.

If motivation and energy is a concern of yours, consider what you might be nutritionally deficient in. You can refer to this book for a list of possible deficiencies that cause lowered energy and motivation, as well as the supplements, natural foods and herbs that **boost** the neurotransmitters which increase energy and motivation.

Long-term improvement develops in small increments overtime. Being proactive will keep that process consistent, and will get you to your goals a lot faster. You will also be able to develop and effectively retain a well-rounded set of interests, skills and hobbies. This habit is vital to boosting your character and core confidence.

8) Additionally, you can **rewire** your brain and body subconsciously with meditation, Hypnosis and Neuro-Linguistic Programming (NLP) to adapt any trait or habit that you want! Your potential for

self-mastery and abundance is infinite! NLP, meditation and Hypnosis have worked effectively for many dedicated and open-minded people to become more outgoing, relaxed, energetic, happier, stronger, sharper and wiser.

You can listen to NLP or Hypnosis audio during a relaxed state or before falling asleep so that your brain can subconsciously register the reaffirmations. You must consistently listen to them at least once a day for a minimum of 6 months for noticeable changes in your perception, mood, attitude, energy and behavior.

You can further seek the support of a NLP Expert, Hypnotherapist, or Healer. There are also several audio products for your own listening.

Chapter 10: Introverts In Love

Finding your way to love (when you would rather stay home and watch Netflix)

When I decided to dip my toe back into the dating pool after a college break-up, I knew I had my work cut out for me. You see, I never enjoyed the dating scene. I spent most of my twenties single by choice. On most nights, I simply preferred to be home, curled up on couch with a book or classic movie, rather than hanging out at the local bars and clubs.

Please don't misunderstand. Like many introverts, I enjoy the company of other people and I love to meet new people. Let me make this point excruciatingly clear: INTROVERTS ENJOY THE COMPANY OF OTHER PEOPLE.

Excuse the all-caps! I simply want to dispel a common myth right off the bat. Many introverts are highly sociable. On any given night, you'll find us singing karaoke, hitting the bar with friends, or hosting killer dinner parties for our friends. Most introverts have a penchant for people-watching, observing, listening and connecting (which makes us great dinner dates). It's just that we also enjoy staying home when we're feeling drained, and taking plenty of alone time to recharge.

The bottom line: just because you enjoy and need solitude to recharge, that doesn't mean you aren't human and won't experience loneliness. All human beings need to establish deep human connections to thrive. For you, this might mean forging friendships, strengthening family relationships, spending time in your religious or spiritual community, and possibly building a long-term relationship with a companion or partner.

Let me explicit when I say I understand that not everyone is looking for a romantic relationship. Maybe you're not in a place in your life right now where that's particularly interesting or appealing to you. But if you're interested in the broad spectrum of romantic life – from flirting to casual dating to establishing a long-term relationship, this chapter is for you. Even if you are in a fulfilling long-term relationship and you're about to celebrate your 25th wedding anniversary (congrats!), there are some tidbits here that can help you gain new insight into the inner workings of your relationship.

Repeat After Me: Dating is Fun

Speed dating, hook-ups, OK Cupid surveys, Tinder swiping, friend zones, friend-with-benefits. When did dating become so complicated? For introverts, the dating scene can sometimes feel like a complicated game that gets old pretty fast. Many of us would rather be in a comfy booth with good friends, enjoying lively conversation and the happy hour cheese plate, rather than setting up nightly blind dates in hopes of making a connection with a random stranger.

But here's the underlying golden rule of thriving in the love and romance department: you won't find love by staying home every night. You have to try. So, if you're ready to jump into the dating pool, here are some tips for squeezing the most fun out of the whole experience.

- Shift your dating mindset. It only takes one terrible blind date to make dating feel like a chore. But, let me re-state the golden rule of the introvert dating cycle: you can't meet great people and make deep connections if you don't leave the house.

Trust me, I know from experience. After a long and protracted break-up, I finally worked up the energy to leave the house and meet a blind date for a cup of coffee. I ended up having coffee with a nice guy named Dave. The date was a bit awkward, but ended sweetly with a hug and a kiss on the cheek.

Now, that nice guy named Dave is my husband. It only took a small gamble – spend an hour having coffee with a friend-of-a-friend – to get on the path that led me to a truly rewarding relationship.

If dating feels like a chore, it's time to make a small but very powerful mind shift. Think of dating as play. Dating puts us in the position to meet new people and have new experiences. Is there a restaurant you've always wanted to try? Invite someone to eat there with you– even if there is no connection, you can at least say you met someone new and checked out that restaurant that was on your list. Take the pressure out of dating by looking at dating as simply a means of learning new things, talking to new people and enjoying new experiences.

- Make connections through the people you trust. Having trouble meeting new people? Yup, been there (more than once). One of the great things about being an introvert is that we tend to enjoy a close and trusted circle of good friends and/or family members. If you're having trouble meeting people – and I know I resisted doing this – ask for help from the people you trust. Chances are, at least one friend (or family member) will know someone who is single. This is an easy way to ease your way into the dating scene. If you're shy or reticent about being set up, remove any pressure by reminding yourself that, hey, it's just a date. Think of this as breaking your dating dry spell, or simply as a way of sharpening your dating mojo.

- Take the reins and plan the first date yourself. Let's say you've lined up a date for Saturday night. If you're like me and you tend to be passive in social situations, do your best to take the lead. Whenever possible, set yourself up for a great night by planning a date where your introvert assets can shine. Most introverts enjoy one-on-one conversations and getting the opportunity to get to know someone on a deeper level. So, make it a point to skip noisy, crowded places. Skip the dance club and crowded bars. What is your idea of a perfect first date destination? A peaceful picnic, dim wine bar, a nature hike? Whatever it looks like, pick a destination where you can easily hold a conversation and get to know your date.

- Avoid group dates. As comforting as it may feel at first to be surrounded by familiar faces, group dates make it hard to connect with a person. Dating is about getting to know someone, and you can't do that if you're in a noisy bowling alley with ten other people. Plan for one-on-one encounters, and save the group dates for later.

- Don't "overbook" yourself. I made this mistake when taking the plunge into the dating pool. In an effort to avoid getting hurt, I decided to date often and planned several dates in a row. This would give me a chance to meet more people and increase my chances of making a connection, right? Not quite. I just ended up feeling tired, overwhelmed and thoroughly confused about what I wanted.

Being flooded with text messages and social commitments is an easy way for any introvert to experience dating drain. Take it at your own pace. That might mean one date a week for some people; for other people, one date a month might be enough. If you feel every muscle in your body groan at the thought of going out on a Saturday night, slow down. Take a break and recharge.

- Be honest about who you are. Growing up, I was always labeled "quiet" and "shy" at school. Many people bristle at labels – I know I did. It can be tempting to want to act like someone else. You might think, "I want to be known as the life of the party. I want to be gregarious, a firecracker, a stud/bombshell, etc…" You are certainly more than an introvert. Like all human beings, you are complex and multifaceted. But you'll save lots of time and energy by being honest about who you are and what you enjoy. If you hate trendy dance clubs, don't pretend to enjoy them for the sake of acting like an extrovert. Risk the chance that you'll be labeled as shy or nerdy. Someone who truly wants to get to know you will know better than to write you off, and will take the time to get to know all of you.

- Remind yourself – daily, if needed – the dating advantage you have as an introvert. Introverts are currently enjoying their moment in the sun (finally!), with loads of new research pointing toward the many benefits that introverts have in the dating scene. Let's count the ways that introverts can crush it in the love department.

First, introverts have an air of mystery about them that can be quite attractive to potential partners. Who is that mysterious girl reading a book alone in the corner booth? Who's that "strong and serious" dude nursing a beer alone at the bar?

Introverts are generally not afraid to appear alone in public. We do things alone, because that's how we recharge. We enjoy our own company. That projects an air of confidence – dare I say sexiness? – that can be quite attractive.

Next, as you know, introverts are deep listeners. And who doesn't enjoy being truly listened to? "Someone who is a good listener" is at the top of many people's dating requirements. No one enjoys the company of self-obsessed blowhards. Count yourself as highly desirable.

Finally, researchers have found that introverts often do well in relationships. Introverts are more likely to listen and be thoughtful when they speak. They are also less likely to speak impulsively during disagreements. Most of us are non-confrontational by nature, preferring to talk things through gently. This inclination often leads to healthier, more loving relationships. Again, crushing it in the love department.

- Skip small talk. We introverts like to get real. And the faster we can get to real, the better. The next time you're on a date, try to skim quickly over run-of-the-mill questions about work and family. Dig deeper by asking about hobbies and future career goals. This will help you avoid getting drained with small talk.

- Date an extrovert. Hey, it worked for me! For years, I did everything I could to meet other introverts. I thought only a fellow introvert would ever truly understand me. While introvert-introvert pairings are a beautiful thing, dating your opposite can also be deeply rewarding.

My husband is a prototypical extrovert. He's the type of person who will strike up a conversation with everyone at the bar. He thrives when meeting new people, socializing and being in the spotlight. It sounds like an odd pairing, but I've benefited so much by sharing my life with someone filled with seemingly endless amounts of social energy. I receive some of the benefits of being an extrovert — getting to meet new people often — without actually forcing myself to act like an extrovert. Yes, there are negotiations involved with dating an extrovert (how long to stay at the Christmas company party, for example), but we complement and balance each other out on so many levels.

- Harness the magic of dating technology. If you have been avoiding online dating, now is the time to get your feet wet. It has never been easier to meet new people – without even leaving the house! Sign up with (insert your preferred online dating service here) today and start browsing the profiles. Most introverts are good written communicators, which is how it all starts in online dating. Send off a quick note to the first person that catches your eye. Next, set up a short phone conversation. Ask yourself: does this person sound like someone I would want to have coffee with? That's all it takes.

Chapter 11: 50 How-Tos In Becoming A Successful Introvert

Office Pin-Up List

1. Challenge assumptions about you in small ways.

2. Observe and learn the on-goings of the office.

3. Keep yourself up to date with the office news and changes.

4. Make an everyday plan.

5. Be proud of your face. This shows confidence.

6. Always be clean, decent and presentable.

7. Smile.

8. Read. Continuous learning has never been deemed useless.

9. Show up early to meetings to show your commitment.

10. Go to regular meetings. Eventually, they will realize what you can do.

11. Be ready. You never know when you need to step out of your comfort zone.

12. Learn people's names.

13. Do not be afraid to jump back in when you are interrupted.

14. Make your work speak for itself.

15. Excel in tasks especially the one that requires less face time.

16. Show seriousness in your work.

17. Consider having an extrovert to support you.

18. Show your self-esteem by volunteering for jobs that you know you can do.

19. Work alone.

20. Take breaks and recharge when necessary.

21. Do not waste time and energy envying the extroverts.

22. Trust the one-on-one conversation system.

23. Become a sounding board for others.

24. Empathize

25. Extend your helping hand.

26. Fill-in for some small tasks.

27. Keep information so people will not consider you expendable.

28. Think of problems as exciting puzzles on you can solve.

29. Do not be afraid to take credit for your work.

30. Reach out to people in the most comfortable fashion to you.

31. Use technology and social media. It is comfortable interaction.

32. Know your worth.

33. Have something that can absorb your anxiety like a pen you can hold.

34. Breathe. No one will put you in prison for responding in a controlled pace.

35. Don't take it personally. It can be difficult for some extroverts to understand your process.

36. Practice small scale networking.

37. Host an event where you can control the environment.

38. See strangers are friends. Everyone is just as scared as you are.

39. Find a similarity between you and another person.

40. Know and research people you want to meet.

41. Practice the three-second rule. Approach people you think are interesting within three seconds to stop you from overthinking.

42. Practice describing yourself within 30 seconds. Some executives do not have time to listen to long speeches.

43. Create a time limit for conversations. Introverts do not like small talks and extroverts have short attention spans to stay in one.

44. Be mindful of body languages—yours and theirs.

45. Take pictures. It lets you're presence known and a perfect excuse for people to talk to you.

46. Use your own style in speaking.

47. Avoid sounding fake or insincere.

48. Give external hints or body language to let people know how you feel.

49. Celebrate your accomplishments no matter how small they are.

50. Always enjoy your alone time.

Monday.

So I'll tell him I'm sorry and explain why I thought his name was Matthew. Maybe I can add that I was having a bad morning? No, I shouldn't. On my period? That could work. No, no. He might act weird with the "P" word. Maybe I can ask Bessie to do it for me? No! You're an independent, self-sufficient woman! You can do it. If it ends badly, then you can just pretend he doesn't exist forever or quit. Good plan.

"Coffee?"

"Yes, thank you." She answered almost immediately and took a sip.

"I could have laced that." Marcus said.

Darn. Over thinking makes her less aware of risks.

"But you didn't" She smiled. If I feel the least bit woozy, I'm stabbing you.

"And for that I've decided to forgive you for not knowing my name."

So I don't have to say it? "Thank you."

"How could you not know my name? I'm great!" He said exuberantly.

Ah. Is it getting a little cramped in here? No, it's just your head getting bigger.

"Maybe I should have the name on my door in huge letters?"

Typical extravert. If it makes you feel better about yourself. "Why not? It will help people like me."

"Maybe later we can go to Henry's Pub for a pint?"

No. I don't think I like you that much.

"What is this 'pub' you speak off?"

"You made a joke... Aw."

This conversation is taking a lot longer than expected. I should have just left the whole thing alone.

"Maybe... but I, uh... sort of promised... my... um..." Now you don't interrupt me?

"Bookshop then?"

Huh. "I'm listening."

"I promise I won't talk to you... I'll just sit on those bean bag things they have in that area of the shop."

"The reading lounge."

"Yes, that one. I'll fend of the creeps lurking around the shop while you browse for hours."

Stay in one place for hours? Wouldn't that kill an extravert? Oh, this could be fun.

"How about you finish those reports and we'll see what happens." I'm sorry but reports need to be finished. I'm just saying.

They both smiled.

You had me at "I won't talk to you."

Chapter 12: Develop And Practice The Skill Of Telling Others What You Need

One of the most difficult things for introverts to tell their family and their significant others is that they would prefer to be alone rather than go out. There are some loved ones who would be understanding, but others would ask: "Why don't you want to go out with us? Is there something wrong?" Of course, what they think of you is not your problem anymore, but you also don't want to damage your relationship with them.

In this case, one of the worst things that you can do is to assume that others should instinctively understand our needs without our having to tell them. Most people are not that sensitive and you will only end up being frustrated. You might even start to take out this frustration on them, which will only make things worse.

Thus, the best thing we can do is to clearly communicate in our preferred fashion that we need time alone or we need our space. You should give your loved ones the assurance that it is not about them, but about you and what you need.

Here are some tips on how to ask for time alone without giving offense:

Explain exactly why you need time alone. Start a conversation with your partner about your need to withdraw to recharge or because you feel overwhelmed. Of course, this can be challenging if your partner has the opposite personality type from you, i.e. they are an extrovert. But if you practice speaking up what you need without sounding frustrated or angry, you'll find that it will work wonders.

Commit to spending time with them at some future date. If you choose to forego a party or social gathering now, you can promise to attend another one later. You should also ensure that this transaction or compromise would not leave you feeling bad or that you are being forced to do something that you don't want to do.

Make sure they understand that your alone time is not about them. An important part of asking for alone time is ensuring that your partner understands that you are not withdrawing because of something they did. You can do this by phrasing your request in such a way as to assure them that your relationship will ultimately be stronger when you get your alone time.

Thus, instead of saying: "We don't have to spend all our time together. I need my alone time, you know," say: "I want to be the best partner that I can be in this relationship and my alone time will help me to be that person".

Assure them that your alone time is not about fixing the relationship. Make sure that your partner and loved ones know that your taking alone time is not because there is something wrong with your relationship with them but about taking care of yourself. Of course, there will always be issues with the relationship that need to be addressed, but instead of looking for problems or taking the blame, you should start by improving your relationship with yourself, and alone time can be an essential part of this.

Chapter 13: Understanding The Psyche Of An Introvert Vs. Extrovert

The discovery of various personalities has triggered some debate on which personality is superior. The answer is neither. Each one of these personalities has its own strengths and weaknesses. Introverts and extroverts should learn to appreciate and respect the differences in each other.

There are many distinctions between introverts and extroverts. These differences mostly stem from the sensitivity of each of these personalities to dopamine and acetylcholine, two powerful neurotransmitters that can affect us both physically and psychologically. Everything from appetite to mood is affected by these neurotransmitters.

Dopamine is a feel-good neurotransmitter, it rewards us with feelings of happiness when we take part in certain activities. Because of this pleasurable feeling, we are spurred to repeat those activities that brought us the feeling of pleasure. Some studies have shown that extroverts have a lesser sensitivity to dopamine, meaning they need more of it to feel happy. Introverts, on the other hand, are more sensitive to dopamine and easily get overwhelmed by activities (such as extreme sports) that lead to an increase in dopamine.

Acetylcholine is also linked to pleasure, but the type of pleasurable feeling it gives is more subtle than that gotten from dopamine. Acetylcholine makes us feel relaxed and focused. It enables us to be reflective, and think. Because extroverts have more dopamine receptors (which in turn make them need higher levels of dopamine to feel good), the pleasure brought about by acetylcholine release is not as intense or desirable to them. They need more external stimulation to feel invigorated and thrive.

Extroverts feel more at home when they're surrounded by many interesting people. It's a lot like sapping energy from a crowd to power up effectively. It is a different story for introverts, however. Not surprisingly, when introverts get too much stimulation from the outside world, they tend to become very stressed and tired. In a way, it's like passing large electrical currents to a very tiny circuit board. The circuit board will eventually burn out in no time. That being said, there are times when introverts and extroverts will need to move out of their comfort zones and try to keep up in different conditions that might seem unsuited to their personality type.

The right mental attitude: Introverts and extroverts

Basically, everyone has an attitude. To a very large extent, attitude defines everything. It influences the way we think, and primarily the way we respond to different situations.

The power of a positive mental attitude is remarkably unlimited. As an extrovert or introvert, you can effectively develop the right mental attitude towards all things: family, work, relationships and society. It all depends on how willing you are to work at it.

Types of Introverts

Introverts have been recently subdivided into four groups. Knowing what type of introvert you are can be instrumental in getting the most out of your life. The four groups are:

The Social Introvert:

This type of introvert doesn't shy away from social events (it should be noted here that shyness and introversion are synonymous). They might enjoy spending time out with friends and acquaintances more than other types of introverts. They usually prefer small groups of people to large groups. They are adept at building meaningful relationships.

The Thinking Introvert:

This type of introvert spends a lot of time in their head. They don't mind being in a crowd, but they'll spend a huge portion of that time lost in their own thoughts. These types are very creative and have a vivid imagination. Thinking introverts can spend too much time in their minds to the detriment of social interactions. Therefore, they should endeavour to set out a specific time for thinking and journaling so that when they're in the company of others, they can enjoy other people's company, knowing they have a set time for thinking alone.

The Anxious Introvert:

These are the type of introverts that feel awkward in social gatherings or in a crowd. They tend to go back home after a social gathering and overanalyze all the things they think they said or did wrong. They worry about how they're perceived by others and this is a major cause of their introversion. Despite the obvious limitation of the overanalyzing introvert, a few strengths of theirs include attention to detail, self-sufficiency and the ability to plan ahead.

The Restrained Introvert:

These introverts think before they act or speak. While the thinking introvert is more creative in thinking, this introvert is more analytical. A unique strength of theirs is seeing the bigger picture. They take some time to make decisions, and notice details people would not normally notice. In order to thrive, these introverts need a while to make decisions.

Chapter 14: The Benefits Of Being An Introvert

No man is an island entire of itself. To be a successful person, people believe one must improve on one's relationship with others. They believe that successful people are only those who have connections with others. In that case, people see the achievement of success as a collective effort. To those people, there is no advantage in keeping oneself away from others. But the question is: are all the successful people extroverts? Has there not been an introvert who has reached the top of the ladder? Perhaps we should not be conclusive in our argument. We may say most of the successful men or women outside there are those who have strong bonds with other extroverts like them, but there are certainly others who do not get along well with so many people but go on to become successful. Although being an extrovert has its advantages, being an introvert is as well not totally disadvantageous. In fact, you should be proud if you are an introvert because of the following benefits you enjoy.

Introverts are Critical Thinkers

Not so many people are good thinkers. In fact, good thinking is a rare commodity. Before one can be a good thinker, one must be a good listener, and introverts are good listeners. No wonder they think wide and critically. There is a benefit in finding more time being alone as that will give one enough space and time to take one's thinking way above others who hardly find time for themselves. Introverts enjoy that privilege to consider and reconsider an issue before coming to a reasonable conclusion. To the introverts, critical thinking comes naturally. The extroverts may find it a bit difficult because they have a lot of others' thoughts competing for their attention. Hence, being a good thinker requires being lonely at times.

Introverts are Geniuses

You are an introvert? Yes, you are a genius! Ingenuity is a byproduct of good thinking. There are not so many ingenious people. If you are the clever type who spends less time than others to think of a practical solution to problems of any kind, people respect you. They respect you not because of anything but because they see you as a valuable asset. When people respect you, it is because they see some qualities in you that distinguish you from them. When people respect you, it is because they see you as a better person. So, being regarded as a genius is a benefit that you as an introvert enjoys over others.

Introverts are Good Observers/ Pay Attention to Details

Instead of being dragged down the tunnel of activities with others, introverts will prefer to sit by and play their observing game. They pay attention to every of the occurrences around them. Every little thing is given an attention by an introvert.

For instance, if an introvert is invited to a party, rather than dancing or running around with others, an introverted person will enjoy his or her time more relishing the activities of others. He or she will prefer to be a bystander in a such a way that if he or she is eventually asked about those around him or her, he or she will be able to say little about them. If introverts make friends, they tend to know their friends more than extroverts know their friends. This is because they are always observant.

Introverts receive care

Being an introvert comes with the benefit of being excessively spoilt with care especially by their partners. A person who has an introvert as a partner will want to go a great length in ensuring that the partner is greatly taken care of. Such a person will be careful in the way he or she treats his or her partner, for he or she knows they have no one else except him or her. Being the sole owner of his or her heart, an introvert's partner will not want to squander such an opportunity. He or she will not want to lose him or her to another person because most people want a quiet partner.

Chapter 15: Silence The Inner Voice

Face Your Fears

If you decide to stay away from other people, you have to do it because of your introvert interests, not because you want to but you feel you are being held back by something. And that something could be a fear you have developed over time.

Without a doubt, years of meeting people and talking to them might not have spared you from disappointments. And these disappointments may grow into fears that keep you from socializing.

Negative interactions from the past could be the ones I am talking about here. For example, if at one time you had a humiliating conversation with a track driver, it's highly likely that you will avoid truck drivers in the future. You will be afraid to go through the same experience. However, people are different. So your fears are unjustifiable.

Another example would be if someone would comment on you while chatting that you are boring. This would be taken as a fact by you. And in every new social situation you may find yourself in, you may be hearing these words playing in your mind.

You need to face all these fears as they may be holding you back. But before you do that, you need to identify each fear and get to its very bottom.

There is no workaround to this but to sit down with a pen and a paper and write down everything you think you hate about going out. This process is not easy.

One trick I like to use is to simply imagine being in a conversation. I try to make it as real as possible. (You may also try remembering social situations from the past that make you shudder.)

Imagine every detail vividly. Pay attention to how you feel as you keep imagining this. What is it that you would change? What are the things you wish you did not say or the other person did not say? Think of what it is that would make you walk away from such situations?

For example, in this exercise, you may find that it is certain topics that you do not enjoy that make you want to walk away. Or it may be how other people respond to you as you talk. You need to get to the very bottom of these things. One way to do that is to use the 5 Whys.

Imagine you are in your favorite café feeling good about life. You look over your shoulder and you see a certain friend about to walk into the same café. All of a sudden, the peace you were enjoying moments ago is overtaken by restlessness. You wish you had walked out of there 2 minutes ago. You start wishing that if you had a magic power, it would be to disappear into thin air.

In moments like these, it is not easy to know why you are feeling a certain way. Your mind gets in a race for solutions. It can't waste time to examine exactly why you are feeling that way. However, you must take time to analyze these feelings. And this is where the 5 Whys come handy. The trick is to ask yourself Why for at least 5 times. After each why, you should be getting closer to the root of your feelings. In this case, it would go like this:

Question: Why do I feel this way?

Answer: I would like to avoid the possibility of meeting (name).

Question: Why does seeing him makes me want to run?

Answer: I hate the way he talks.

Question: Why do I hate the way he talks?

Answer: He likes to brag about how much fun he always has by going to parties or drinking.

Question: Why does that bother me?

Answer: He makes me feel like I am locked in a box and I need to come out. He pushes me to act more like him.

Question: What's wrong with acting like him?

Answer: I know that my personality would not manage to live the way he does. I am an introvert.

Of course, your answers may be different from mine. But I am sure you get the idea. In some situations, especially if you provide the wrong answers, you may not be able to uncover the real thing that's bothering you. That's why it is really important to ponder over each question. Ask yourself if your answer justifies the feelings you feel. And more importantly, always try to look for other possible explanations.

Once you have uncovered the things that create fears, you then need to create solutions. Of course, the solution will depend on the problem in question. For example, if it is certain subjects that annoy you, then try to keep your conversations from drifting into those directions.

For some fears, however, there is nothing you can do by accept them. Sometimes, simply accepting facts to be the way they are can do wonders for you.

Don't Judge Yourself

You are your own waste critic. It is unhelpful to go around thinking others are judging you in the same way you are judging yourself. People are too busy with their lives and their problems. So don't give a damn about their thoughts. You will waste your time. And you will rob yourself the chance to enjoy the present moment you are in.

You can think of this behavior as having a mirror everywhere you go in front of you. And you use this to evaluate your look, the way you talk, how you walk, and more. Instead of listening to what others are saying, you get busy finding flaws in yourself. Women make the majority of people with this problem.

However, there is a simple trick you can use. And that is to practice what I call mindful observation. Instead of focusing on your flaws, simply focus on others or the environment you are in.

You may observe the colors of paints in your surroundings or inquire about the flowers you see about.

If in a conversation, try to paint pictures of what the other is saying in your mind. Actually, this will help you understand the other person better. You will ask questions mindfully and will show your full interest in the conversation.

By doing this, there is no time for you to worry about yourself.

Don't Fear Failure

The fear of failure is another problem most introverts have to deal with. However, it is not that we fear the failure itself. The fear is more to do with failing in public. We think of the embarrassment we will suffer in such situations. And that only makes us fear getting in public even more.

The thing is humans do not like to make themselves feel vulnerable. And as a result, we like to protect ourselves from situations we consider dangerous, even if these situations may bring us benefits we need.

But the problem is that if you do not put yourself out there, you do not get to face the thing that you fear. So the fear still remains. However, the more you expose yourself to something, the more you become comfortable with it.

There is a little trick that can change how you see failures – and that is to think of how far they will take you down. If you try to make friends and fail, your world will not end. And you can try making more friends in future. By that time, however, you will be in a much better position with all the experience you will gain.

Let Go of Rejections

As I already said, people are usually too busy with their own lives to waste time thinking about you. So as you go out there, you need to be mindful of one thing – you will face rejections. This does not mean you are not likable or interesting. People have their own baggage of problems.

You may say "hi" to someone and he may respond coldly. That may be because he had a fight with his wife and he would simply like to have some time to himself.

Rather than taking such things personally, recognize them as unsuccessful attempts and move on. But they should not in any way stop you from making new friends wherever you go.

Chapter 16: Let Your Creativity Flourish

Another selling point of being an introvert is that you are able to express whatever is currently in your head. Most introverts are known to wield the powers of an artisan, one who is able to create magnificent works of art. We are not really talking about just the visual arts, but we are also delving into the spheres of music, sculpture and literature.

As evidenced by the output of such individuals as Picasso and Stephen King, introverts do possess an inclination towards beautiful and meaningful things.

Consider yourself lucky when you count as one among countless of talented stars that shine bright in the artistic universe. Because you are able to see inside the ideas that you nurture in your head, you are also able to wield just about the right amount of clarity to empty out your brain and produce truly magnificent works of art.

Want to bring out the creative in you? Here are some important ways to go about it.

Make room for hobbies

Introverts tend to be looked upon as isolated individuals with peculiar tastes in terms of seeking fun and excitement. We are also made to believe that introverts care little about free time. It isn't so, since most introverts prefer to spend idle time on interests considered boring among the more snobbish extroverts.

Hobbies play a major role in stimulating introverts' curiosity. Usually, they spend significant amounts of time solving puzzles like Sudoku, or engage in highly entertaining online games. There are also those who tend to burn a little time by writing poems, sketching and photography. Introverts always have an eye for the beautiful as much as they have an eye for things with organic or inorganic meaning, and this is the kind of stimulation that introverts truly enjoy.

You might want to bring a sketchpad outside and draw whatever the scenery provides. During rainy days, you might try to cordon yourself in the bedroom and listen to the sound of droplets inviting you to write a poem about them. Or if you are up for a little adventure, go hiking up a hill or mountain you always wanted to conquer, reach the peak and take a snapshot of the vast view that will last a lifetime.

There is inspiration everywhere and it makes perfect for an introvert to use his ability to absorb his surroundings and produce a replication of what he finds as beautiful.

Spend time with creative people

One thing's for sure, as an introvert, you basically shun any form of socialization even if it means being inspired by it. Well, it does sound a good idea when you choose the kind of people you want to be with.

It's not that I am teaching you how to discriminate people based on their Myers-Briggs personality test results. But there is some truth to the saying that "birds of a feather, flock together." Therefore, there's nothing to lose when you start to talk with like-minded people. Rubbing elbows with the right personalities enables you to open up new galaxies of inspiration. You are able to exchange ideas, absorb new knowledge and apply new concepts to the things that interest you.

 Go on cultural excursions

Here, you don't necessarily go on casual trips to the museum during the weekend. What this entails is to go wherever there is culture. Whether you plan on going on a trip to some remote village or attend a music festival featuring Australian Aboriginal folk music, the world is basically your oyster for cultural awareness.

Being open to other cultures allows you to open up your creative mind. It also gives you an opportunity to learn new things that your knowledge hungry mind wants to bite into. So if you know some sort of cultural event in your community, do not hesitate to join in and discover just how much there is to know about the world. Besides, you diary needs some interesting content to satiate its pages.

Make stories out of the everyday

What's the best thing about being an introvert? Well, you are as observant as a super detective. You tend to have this ability to assess people based on the way they dress, speak and walk. It's a gift. Though not exactly mutant in nature, but introverts are just so detail-oriented that they are able to generate intricate backstories for the people they see in the park for example. Which is why introverts make for the best writers – they are so interested in people that they choose to be on the sidelines and make up interesting stories.

Writing has its perks here, so as an introvert, you better convince yourself to publish a novel based on the people you meet. Not that it should mirror real-life, but at least it gives a semblance of people are rendered through your own unique perspective. For Jack Kerouac, sketching the lives of people is in itself a service to the arts. You are practically replicating what you see onto your own little canvas.

There are as many stories as there are people, and in case you take the literary route, might I suggest starting at a café? Order your favorite brew, sit down, and observe the people that are casually having their espressos with their cheesy conversations. You will surprised by how much material it entails to fill a 400-page novel!

Be inspired everyday

It might sound like a long shot, but inspiration as we know it is found everywhere. It's only a matter of going to where it usually settles. On the other hand, it's something more of a hit-or-miss endeavor. You do not exactly know where inspiration rests, but there is a good chance you would encounter it. Call it luck, but people have better odds when they start to take action.

Instead of lazing around all day, browsing memes, try to discover the good things about being an introvert by actually looking for inspiration instead of waiting for it to come. A successful man is one who believes in action and shuns illusions after all.

In essence, being an introvert is actually more about being a creative individual. Invoking the creativity in you won't be farfetched, just as long as you lead an authentic life that lives and breathes art.

Chapter 17: Dealing With Your Social Fears

Are you afraid of being in a large group of people? Do you feel anxious when you are about to meet new people?

Understanding the Problem

If this is the case, you need to find out why. You also need to identify the specific aspects of being in a crowd and meeting new people that make you anxious. There is a pattern on how the fear or anxiety builds up. For most people, it starts with a trigger. Your fear may start when you hear that you need to attend the social events. Some introverts only hate social events when they did not expect it. Others become fearful when they need to take part in a social activity that focuses attention to them. This fear is usually related to performance in the social setting.

Fear is normal. It is a natural way for our body to warn us of danger. However, it can be socially debilitating, especially if fear creates a habit of preventing us from doing our duties.

Let's take Mike for example. Mike is about to spend his **3rd** Christmas in the company. He did not attend the two first Christmas parties of the company because there are always activities where he can get embarrassed. He tries to talk himself into going to the activity but his fear always wins. In the past two years, he always decides, on the last minute, to stay home and make up some excuse on why he can't make it.

In the past two holiday parties, Mike did not understand why he does not want to go. However, as he analyzed the pattern of fear, he realized that it was performing in the crowd that made him anxious. He enjoyed the idea of having a good time with his colleagues and he even looks forward to talking to some of the people. However, whenever the idea of performing in front of his coworkers pops in his mind, he begins to feel anxious. He starts imagining scenarios wherein he becomes embarrassed.

By knowing the specific part of the party that Mike fears, he may be able to avoid the performance part instead of avoiding the whole event altogether.

Triggers are thoughts of social activities that start the fear in your mind. When the fear starts, a socially anxious person begins a series of activities that will lead him to avoid certain social activities. In the professional world, missing certain events and activities may be interpreted as not being a team player.

To prevent your social fear from stopping you from doing something, you need to identify the specific cause of your fear. Here are some of the common social activities that people fear:

• Speaking in public
• Doing something while a huge crowd is watching
• Being teased or laughed at

• Presenting in front of people with authority

• Being on a date or meeting someone you are romantically interested in

• Giving a performance on stage

• Starting a casual conversation

In most cases, most people realize that the things they fear the most are not important and that they can actually fight it. However, some introverts never find the willpower to fight their fears even when they know that the scenario they fear may not actually happen. Here are some of the things that you can do to prevent your fear from taking over your actions:

Control How you Think to Deal with your Fears

There are certain thinking patterns that socially anxious individuals often use. Here are some of them:

• Assumptions and predictions

People who are anxious assume that there are always opportunities in events for them to become embarrassed. They make a lot of assumptions that lead to their fears. They also make predictions on how things will happen. For people with social anxiety, this becomes a habit.

When you begin assuming and predicting fearful scenarios, it is a signal that you need to distract your mind from the fear. People have different coping mechanisms against fear. If you are in the office when the fear happens for example, you can occupy your mind with work to prevent it from ruling over your thoughts.

• Extreme negative thinking

The assumptions and predictions of introverts who have social anxiety are usually worsened by their extreme negativity. When thinking of these events, they focus on the worst things that may happen.

• Personalizing

When thinking of the things that can go wrong in the social events, they also focus on how the people in the party will react towards them. They think that people are out to make fun of them. They imagine that the bosses are there to humiliate them.

• The flight or fight response

When the fear starts, stress hormones will then activate their flight or fight response. For socially anxious introverts, the automatic response is to avoid the event. They may have made the choice not to attend the event in the past and they turned out all right. Whenever they faced the same type of stress after that, they decided to use the same response to the stress.

Over time, these patterns of thinking become automatic when they are required to attend events that they are not familiar with. Continued use of these patterns of thinking and behavior prevents a person from enjoying social success.

How to Prevent Social Fears?

Breathing exercises

Breathing is one of the few functions that our body performs with both the conscious and subconscious mind. Being able to control the subconscious acts of breathing by being conscious of them is a powerful tool. One of the first signs of anxiety is an increased pace of shallow breaths. This may happen when you are about to go to the event. It may also happen even when thinking of the event. When you feel this happening, you should try to take back your control of your breathing. For example, when you feel that you are becoming nervous or fearful about a certain social situation, you should find a chair and do the following breathing exercise:

1. Sit and relax on the chair with your back straight and your face forward. Put your right hand on your right lap and your left hand on the surface of your stomach.

2. Slowly take a deep breath through your nose while expanding your stomach as the air comes in. Take at least 4 seconds to

inhale. Hold the air in for 2 seconds before you slowly exhale it. Exhale through your mouth. It should take more than 4 seconds for you to exhale all the air out.

3. You should do this for 2 minutes or until you feel relaxed. By the time you are done, any fast-paced shallow breathing should be gone.

Change anxiety-related behavior with actions related to countering your fear

For most people, the flight response becomes a habit after the trigger. In the beginning, a socially anxious introvert may still try to convince himself to go to the event. Over time, the person no longer considers going. Every time an idea of attending an event makes him feel uncomfortable, he automatically decides not to go.

You can change such habit even if you have been practicing it for years. All you have to do is to identify the trigger of your fear and explain in detail the behavior that follows it. You should then identify the rewarding feeling that you get when you decide not to attend an event because of fear.

Now that you have identified that cycle of your habit, you need to associate bad feelings towards the habit. Think of the negative effects of the habit. Make a list of it so that you can remind yourself of the negative effects that the habit has done for you. This will convince your subconscious mind that the habit is not doing any good for you.

Next, you need to think of a behavior change in response to the trigger. As mentioned above, first comes the trigger. It is then followed by the routine of the habit. The trigger feeling and the fear will always be there. You cannot change that. You can change the behavior that follows the fear. Let's say you always avoid your family holiday dinners because of some embarrassing experience. Every time you think of the event, you feel embarrassed inside. Over time, this feeling has developed into fear that the same experience will happen in the future.

You need to decide to go. You must not argue with yourself or waiver between the decision of going or not. When you have decided that you will go to the next one, your next challenge will be the thoughts that will bring back memories of your dreaded embarrassing experience. To prevent it from affecting your decision, you should look for a way to change your behavior every time memories of the experiences enter your mind.

Instead of thinking too much about it, you can say the phrase "I'm going" and think of another thought. Every time your fear of social events creeps in, you should say this phrase. Verbalizing it creates a sense of strength in most people. It symbolizes the change in habit that will bring them back to attending social events for good.

Lastly, you should identify the trigger as it happens. Every time you feel the fear, start anticipating the behavior that follows. You should then use the phrase used above or any variation of it to prevent your mind from going into the habit.

Expose your mind to your fear

One of the best ways to deal with fear is to face it. You may feel overwhelmed if you face all of your fears all at once. A better strategy is to face them one at a time. Instead of going to all the social events that you are invited to, you should focus your mind to only one. Once you have attended that event, you should think of the next one that you will attend. You should assure yourself that the worse case scenario that you think up in your head is always your irrational fear speaking and will probably not happen.

After attending dozens of social events, you will begin to enjoy the experience. You will start to develop courage when you fear something about an event. As you go to more events, the habit of going to them begins to develop. Once that habit develops that's when the magic happens and your confidence take a noticeable turn for the best. The key is changing your habits.

Chapter 18: Develop Into A More Sociable Introvert

You may have not heard of the word "sociable introvert" because it sounds so contradictory. But you can get out of your comfort zone and be more outgoing and companionable, despite the popular, and very untrue, notion that introverts are antisocial.

Before you can create a successful mindset, you need to recognize and accept the traits you have as an introvert:

They prefer little stimulation, social or physical.

They are not always shy.

They enjoy spending time with people, too – just not too many.

They would rather work alone and avoid crowds, bright lights or noise.

They process information differently.

They love predictability, making plans and routine.

As an introvert, you must first discover what causes you the most anxiety or discomfort. Outside your comfort zone, there is a place where you feel a limited anxiety which can actually make you more productive.

For example, most introverts will do very well in the beginning of a new job even though it is unnerving for them. The reason behind this is that they want to prove themselves and will give extra effort, commitment and attentiveness to the job. On the other hand, other introverts will feel overwhelmed if they don't meet the skill sets or training required for the job and this can affect their productivity.

It is not easy to discover your optimal anxiety zone. You need to closely monitor yourself and determine where your anxiety overshadows your productivity. Tap into your potential so you can overcome your apprehensions.

Here are 10 ideas to help you overcome social ineptness and bashfulness and become more sociable:

You should challenge yourself.

When you push yourself past areas of comfort, you will realize that you are giving yourself the opportunity to learn new things and accomplish more than you thought was possible. It doesn't mean that you will become an extrovert overnight. You also need to take it slowly and not push yourself too much that you will be on the verge of a breakdown. When you push yourself out too soon, too much, you are creating more anxiety for your life. Take it one day, one step at a time.

Learn to start small.

As you progress with small achievements, you will build confidence to try out new and more daring things – whether it is talking to a bigger group of people or trying out more adventurous cuisine.

Be spontaneous.

Introverts are prone to planning and taking their own sweet time to think things through. Now you don't have to drop everything and be totally impulsive to the extent that you become irresponsible. Start with small goals such as going on an unplanned vacation or a spur-of-the-moment party. You can also invite a friend or co-worker to have lunch with you. Take your spouse or partner on an impromptu date. Try spontaneity in safe situations so that you can enjoy the rewards and feel more confident in the future.

Join a social group

Practice meeting new people and you'll get better at it. You might want to get started by joining Toastmasters. Remember that growth requires you to venture out of your comfort zone regularly. Toastmasters will enable you to that because you'll be meeting a lot of new people and even practice speaking in front of a crowd during meetings.

Eventually, you'll become more comfortable speaking in front of a crowd, if not get used to it.

Remember that you don't have to go to bars or night clubs to make new friends.

When you want to come out of your shell and make friends, you can look for social situations where you can encounter new people. You can even make your own social setting. For instance, set up a small get-together in your home and invite your friends to bring another friend. This way you will be in a relaxing social setting and get the chance to talk with people you haven't met before.

Go face-to-face.

There is nothing wrong with online friendships or relationships but you need to take it up to a personal level. Meet offline so that people don't have to be total strangers to you even as you chat with them online.

You can join a yoga class or a workout group.

You can still tend to your introvert tendencies while having other people around you.

Go to a book club.

If there is none in your area, start one. Reading is one of the most loved activities of an introvert and a book club can make it a social activity. You will be able to meet new people who share your interest and exchange opinions. Book clubs do not meet frequently so it is a good way for introverts to go out and socialize without getting too drained.

You can take up an acting class.

Did you know that Robert De Niro and Emma Watson are introverts? Yet they are very good actors. You will learn how to take on a different character in a safe environment and be able to explore, understand and act out different behaviors without being judged. It will help you push past your introvert tendencies.

Be involved with a musical group.

When you take part in a musical group, you will not only enjoy a hobby and learn a new thing, you will also be able to make friends who share you love for music. There is no pressure to socialize because the group will be focused on the music – but it is a good way to get yourself out there.

It is not true that extroverts are the only ones who are good at socializing. While they take initiative and are more positive about social interactions, many introverts can also seek out interactions and be good communicators.

Today, make an effort to flex those social skills. You don't have to work the room – just try to speak to one person when you are in a party. If you are feeling daunted, you can search out another wallflower like you and strike up a conversation by introducing yourself. They may be as introverted as you and it could be the beginning of a friendship.

Get up and get out there. There is no harm in trying – you have nothing to lose and everything to gain.

Chapter 19: How To Raise An Introverted Child

Imagine this scene from everyday life. You are arriving to pick up your five-year son from a birthday party; his little friends are running and playing around. You are greeted by an unexpected sight: while other children are happily running around the yard with birthday boy, your son is in a corner of the yard in the company of the birthday boy's mother pampering the family dog, and he seems very happy. Or you come to kindergarten to pick up your daughter, and she is, instead of participating in group play, sitting alone in the corner of the room looking through a colorful picture book.

It is possible that these sights cause you anxiety, because you have a picture of your child as a highly social and open child (maybe even as a "leader of the pack"), or secretly believe that because of the enjoyment of such independent activities he is doomed to life full of sadness and loneliness.

To "fix" the situation, you organize a social life for your child (in the form of everyday socializing, gaming, social activities), and you're wondering why he is nervous, tearful and upset. At the same time, from different parties you receive reliable information about how your child really enjoys having fun and playing with his close friend or cousins, and how he even more enjoys being in a small group of peers and without any problem fits in his kindergarten group. Is there really cause for concern? Answer: no, because you probably share your life with a child who could be characterized as introverted.

Parents who love being in the spotlight often undermined the confidence of their introverted child trying to adapt them to their own values. The same goes for introverted parents who do not accept their introversion as they were feeling bad when they were kids so they do not want it for their children. From the children, we usually expect that they are happy, in a good mood and playful since "That is what children should be." Rarely do parents think that their nature may be different and that they also have the right to belong to extroverted or introverted personality type.

1.1. Why are we trying to make our introverted kid into an extrovert?

1.Mixing shyness and introversion

As I have already stated introversion and shyness are not the same. In fact, while the shy person avoids other people and in the background of such behavior is often a lack of confidence or fear of criticism, introverted do not care much what others think about their behavior. Hence the prejudices that introverted children and people are rowdy. However, they simply do not pay much attention to politeness since they don't consider it essential for a quality relationship.

2.General environment

The modern world has imposed certain ideals as a desirable value. Most adults believe that in this tough world those who are successful must know how to be proactive, which is the main motive for parents to try to change some features of their children. They have the best intentions, forgetting that their best intentions are sometimes not the best solutions for the child. Parents often use verbal violence and sneering to "wake up" their introverted child that is devastating. In this way, parents create an insurmountable gap in communication with their introverted child.

2. Is it possible to change an introverted child into extroverted?

Have you ever thought that the extroversion or introversion is actually inherited trait? Jerome Kagan, a developmental psychologist at Harvard, was dedicated to researching just introversion and in 1989 he performed an important experiment. By studying five hundred babies aged four months, he found that 20 percent of them are highly sensitive. The reactions have been observed about external events such as the burst of the bubble or the smell of alcohol. Kagan concluded that those babies tend to grow up to be introverted children, and then introverted adults. Years later, he found that toddlers who were highly sensitive in the early period "retain" those same responses as teenagers too. In this way, he confirmed his initial assumption that babies who were introverted at the age of four months remain with this feature even when they grow into teenagers. So the sooner you accept introversion of your child, it will be easier for both of you.

3. Extroverted parents and introverted children

If one of the parents is an introvert, the child is usually introverted too, which contributes to a better understanding. However, when one or both of the parents are extroverted, the extroverted parent usually tries to make the child adapt to being extroverted too. In such cases, educators and child psychologists occupy a unique position, and recommend gentle guidance which includes:

The true measure

For a child, it is important to feel welcome in the family, with the whole package of its characteristics, strengths and weaknesses. Never let him be under impression that he is not good enough to be accepted by you, because he doesn't meet your expectations. It will collapse his confidence, ruin your relationship and make him even more "closed" in himself. Instead, try to navigate, correct and encourage your child, but not beyond his personal capabilities, more in an appropriately dosed extent.

Encourage her in what is important to her

Support "in the back" will further "open" your introverted child and strengthen her in the areas that you think are important.

A child needs praise from parents regardless of whether it is "withdrawn" or "loud". Research shows that babies who were commended in the first year of life grow up to be optimistic people. Based on the initial impression of the baby that the world is mostly pleasant or unpleasant place, we can predict whether a baby will later in life become an optimist or a pessimist. If you meet your baby's needs, both physiological (feeding, dressing, bathing ...) and psychological (cooing, cuddling, embrace ...), you significantly influence on what kind of person it will grow up to be regardless of the classification into introverted and extroverted.

Respect the nature of your child

Always respect the child's difference. Do not push him to be like you if you are extroverted, your child is entitled to his values, wishes, and ambitions. Keep in mind that your job as a parent is to direct, instead of trying to change the child's character.

Social contacts

The big concern, especially of extroverted parents, is that their introverted child will not have many friends. They think that the child with a reduced number of contacts will forever be lonely. If your child does not associate with a large number of peers, it also means that the relationships that it builds are much deeper and longer. After all, your child may not have 3,000 friends on Facebook, but would that be some evidence of success?

Support

Help him at an early age to cultivate relationships with peers by teaching him basic social characteristics, so he could satisfy his needs for a companionship with a small but select number of friends. It is your job to direct him towards the company and try to turn him on sports clubs or activities. It is your job to show him options and to support him, and he will find out what his interests are.

4. For who is better that your child is an extrovert: for you or him?

Prejudice

Introversion is neither diagnosis nor disorder. Introvert does not mean that your child is sad or condemned to a life without pleasures.

Equal achievements

Numerous studies and experiments show that both extroverted and an introverted person can achieve the same academic success, if that is what concerns you as a parent.

Benefits

Introverts deeply reflect on the decision, which means they usually make the right decision, as I have already stated. They are successful in focusing on a specific problem, which contributes to the fact they come up with new, sometimes revolutionary ideas and solutions.

A sense of personal happiness

Finally, there are studies that show that introverted people often describe themselves as happy, and extroverted people see themselves as partially happy. Here's something to think about, especially those parents who suffer because their child is introverted. Is not a happy child what we all desire?

I think that the research show this because in an introverted person the feeling of happiness is based more on self-reliance while extroverts are constantly looking for some external stimulation.

1.2. How to develop self-confidence and self-awareness in introverted children

Introvert children often wonder what and how to do things, think about who they are and ask themselves a lot of question. In this way, an image of oneself is created that can last a lifetime. By asking themselves these and other contemplative questions, the children seek answers to who they are and try to create an experience of the world, a way of communicating with the world and way to understand them better. It is true that introverted children are more sensitive than extroverted because they are constantly "in their head". No one says you have to act overprotective towards them, but you should bear in mind their can by hypersensitivity, which is not a bad trait.

Children compare with each other in kindergarten, school, sports clubs, with friends and within different groups to which they belong and thus realize their values and abilities. Evaluation of themselves in relation to others brings them both positive and negative information about themselves so they know exactly what are their strengths, and what are their weakness. Self-confidence and self-awareness began to develop through 'self-evaluation.

It is essential that we do not identify the terms self-confidence and self-awareness because they are different and do not have the same meaning, but are closely linked. It is important to distinguish these terms, but also to develop them in children.

Self-confidence is a measure of what we are capable of doing, at what we are good or bad, what we can and what we can't do and what are our capabilities and skills.

Self-awareness is the knowledge that we have about ourselves and experience of who we are, what we think of ourselves and how we can relate to that knowledge.

A child may be good at math, but not in the sport. The better child is at math; his confidence in this field is growing. However, that gives us a child that is good at math, but it does not mean it will help him to be good in basketball. Therefore, it is important that we develop healthy self-awareness and that the child knows to deal with their failures. The enhanced self-esteem of the child means that the child has a good self-image. Self-confidence is related to the child's achievement while the self-awareness is related to the child's existence.

A parent can help the child develop self-confidence if the child is objectively praised for all his accomplishments and parents regularly give them feedback on his or her abilities and skills. A huge role in the development of self-esteem in a child, the parent has in helping him to develop a sense of competence. A large number of introverted children are often accompanied by an unrealistic sense of their capabilities; they think they are not capable or less capable than others and that even though they practice or train they will fail. Therefore, it is essential parental guidance in the right direction with support and encouragement.

Self-awareness can be seen as an internal pillar that we can keep stable, secure, "good in our own skin," but it can be unstable and then we feel guilty, unhappy and insecure.

Why is the self-awareness essential?

A child who has a well-developed self-awareness is less vulnerable, has better relationships with other children and adults, is happier and enjoys life more. A parent needs to help the child to develop the quantitative and qualitative dimension of self-awareness.

Do we like company or solitude, do we like to speak in front of a large group or not, whether we are sensitive to injustice or we are not bothered by that. The qualitative dimension is the awareness of how we handle the facts we know about ourselves, in this way we will be able or not to separate the failures of us as individuals. This is very important because then the child will be able to say: "I got a bad grade because I did not learn, but that does not mean I'm stupid and that I cannot learn that subject."

In developing self-confidence of the child, important reactions of parents to the child can usually go in two directions:

1.The direction in which we accept and respect our kid just the way it is with all its positive and negative sides.

2.The direction of insults, accusations and rejection because it is not the way we imagined it should be.

It is certain that the first line is the right choice to react to the child because it will allow him to develop a healthy and good self-esteem. If we accept both positive and negative sides of the child, the child will also accept and love himself just the way it is.

How can we recognize whether our introverted child has problems with self-confidence? The most common signs are:

1.The child is too quiet and shy

2.She is too self-critical and cries a lot

3.He shows a great distrust towards other people

4.She has a need to pamper other people

5.He apologizes for everything he did

6.She feels fear when trying something new and is too hard for her to make a decision or a choice.

How can parents help?

Parents should by all means show their unconditional love, children need to feel and experience parents' love when they successfully deals with things, and when they are doing something wrong.

Be honest with your child. Children always feel our honesty or dishonesty, especially those children who are more contemplative than others. What we are talking, must be seen also in our eyes, body, and voice. Look and listen to your child, talk to him "face to face" and really hear what he is telling you. Try more to understand his current situation and his feelings.

When you praise and when you criticize be specific, let your child know exactly what you mean, do not use some general phrases.

When criticizing, never criticize the personality of the child, just the behavior. e.g. "It is not right that you have taken your brother's things" instead of "You are bad". If your child is having trouble in school do not say "You have to begin to learn, you know you've got to fix it," but use a different approach, like, "I see that something is wrong, do you have problems in school? I wish you can tell me something about it. Can I help you? "When a child feels your sincere interest in him, he will turn to himself, reflect on and seek a solution to the new situation.

A parent should not only help a child to develop self-confidence and self-awareness but must show to his child by personal example how to love himself. Finally, it is important to say that parents should not forget that two-way education process, parents provide lessons to children, but also children give lessons to parents. Being a parent means that you need to enrich constantly and develop as a person.

1.3. Whether your child is introverted or withdrawn for some other reasons?

Despite the fact that introversion in children is not considered to be an advantage, it isn't a disadvantage for the child. How will our children feel, largely depends on how we as parents treat their isolation.

First of all we must understand that the introversion trait is not a disadvantage. Many people we know in whose company we feel comfortable are also introverted. Such people are often good "listeners" and peaceful people who are well adjusted in society.

If your child's temperament is quiet and withdrawn, that is introverted, never say to other people things like, "He is withdrawn," especially if the child is nearby. It sounds a bit like an excuse, and that is not needed.

There is nothing wrong in seclusion, on the contrary. Many people do not understand the reticence and think of it as a problem. They believe that the child suffers from a lack of confidence which is, in most cases, completely wrong and unfair to the child. Many withdrawn children have strong views about themselves, have an inner peace that shines and if open and "talkative" people could be quiet long enough they would see their luster.

Many parents are worried when a child runs away from a noisy crowd and raise the question of whether the child is just withdrawn or is there a problem that's bothering them? How to distinguish these two things? Observe your child when and how he communicates with others.

In fact, withdrawn child with a developed sense of self-confidence makes eye contact with other people in their vicinity and seems satisfied. Such children behave mostly polite, pleasant, and people feel good in their vicinity.

Many withdrawn children are thoughtful and slower and more cautious in developing communication with strangers. They study a new person in their environment and question whether they are worth the effort of establishing a relationship. These children are careful in making friendships, but when they find a friend, it is usually a good and lasting friendship. Their reticence can be explained like aloofness and thoughtfulness, which are by no means negative traits.

Withdrawal as a reflection of internal problems

With some children reticence reflects their internal problems and such children are more than just quite. Such children are unsafe, avoid direct eye contact and have behavioral problems. Other peers do not feel comfortable in their vicinity.

When you carefully observe such children, you will find that they are full of fear, uncertainty, and possibly anger. Instead of peace and trust, you will find in them unrest and distrust. If you notice this in your child's behavior, try to find out what causes such feelings and try to resolve it together.

Withdrawal as a mask

It is possible that some children hide behind the "retreat" in order not to allow the others to discover what they do not like in themselves. The label "seclusion" becomes an excuse for not developing their social skills and a reason to avoid the company of peers.

In these children, withdrawal is arising from an underdeveloped sense of self-esteem. Such a child has self-critical thoughts such as "I'm no good" or" I can do nothing well." Such a child is prone to become passive, very much withdrawn, or even depressed. When confronted with a new challenge, this child with low self-esteem will think, "I cannot do it."

If you notice that your child has a poor self-image and that it feels insecure, then you should in every way try to strengthen its self-confidence and self-esteem to help him to be equally involved in society. Such a child needs parents who can be trusted, on which he can always rely to treat him in a way that will diminish a sense of insecurity, frustration, and inner rage.

Puberty and behavioral changes

By entering puberty, many children become dissatisfied with themselves, uncertain and too self-critical. Before you tell your relatives for such behavior of your child, or consult a psychologist, be patient. Encourage your child and give him time to re-open to the world.

Parents often wonder what to do with the withdrawn child. Is this just a passing phase? Do you encourage your child to be more open? Is there a deeper problem?

Some more tips on how to behave if a child is withdrawn:

1.Acceptance

It is important to understand that you have a sensitive and withdrawn child who is slowly making contacts with strangers.

2.Be careful what you say

If your child is withdrawn because she suffers from a lack of self-confidence and hasn't developed self-awareness yet, then make sure you do not hurt her with your words. Children are very sensitive to the words of their parents and important adults who they respect and value.

Remember that a child should be praised for his efforts to carry out certain jobs, not only for the successful completion of the project. Take care not to exaggerate, or to speak untruth. For example, if the child did not achieve its goals, avoid sentences like "Next time you'll work harder, and you will certainly succeed." I would rather say something like "It did not turn out as you hoped, but I'm very proud of the effort you put into it."

Be spontaneous and full of love. Your love can certainly boost a child's confidence.

Hold the child, kiss him, and show him how proud you are of him, not only because of his success but mostly because of who he is. Compliment him often and sincerely, but without exaggeration. Children have a great ability to sense when something comes "from the heart."

You can't be a positive model to your child if you have low self-esteem because if you are self- critical, pessimistic, or unrealistic about your capabilities and limitations, there is a strong likelihood that your child will eventually "copy" or to develop a system of self-realization and behave in accordance with what he learned by watching and listening to you. Take care of yourself, as this will get your child a positive role, model.

3.Don't force the support

We want to "help" to a withdrawn child, but usually this sort of endeavor has an opposite effect. It is much better to create a safe environment in which children can naturally develop their sociability.

Never criticize your child because he is withdrawn and quiet and do not allow him to think that is something's wrong with that. If you are going to visit relatives, do not tell him in front of them not to be shy or explain him to them like "He/she is like that". It's much better before starting to explain to your child what behavior you expect from him, according to his capabilities.

When you are in a company and you notice that your child is feeling uncomfortable because the focus of attention is on him, try to move discreetly to another topic.

4.Without pressure

Sometimes you wish that your withdrawn child demonstrates his talents and successes in front of your friends or relatives. Do not push him into the spotlight without warning. If you want your child to play some instrument or show any other talent in front of relatives or friends, ask him. Allow room for him to reject your wishes if discomfort is stronger than the desire to please you.

If your child is expecting a public appearance, help him overcome this skill gradually. If he plays some instrument, let him first make music in front of you or your closest friends.

5.Withdraw

Allow the child to express him and do not choke it with your eloquence. When someone asks something, do not answer for him. If you are talkative and extrovert, your child can be even more withdrawn in your company.

1.4. Are you overprotective toward your introverted child?

Some parents are doing the same mistake in raising introverted children by being overprotective which in no case can be a good thing. If you are acting this way towards your introverted child you are not doing him a favor at all.

The basic postulate of every development, including child's, is defeating obstacles and challenges. As in adults, in children occurs sense of achievement after successfully mastering the challenges that give rise to confidence. We are all very aware that confidence is one of the basic requirements for success in any field of life. Problems in the development of the child's self-esteem arise whether when obstacles are insurmountable, or when a child does not have to overcome it. In a child who does not have any obstruction to overcome comes to a pathological personality development. We say these kids are overprotected by their parents or close family members.

Overprotected child grows in the constant presence of two messages: that he is not capable and that this world is a very dangerous place. These messages form the idea of self, others, and the world, so instead of growing into an active and independent adult, it grows into a passive and dependent one. Passive because he does not dare doing anything out of fear he is incompetent, and that the world is very dangerous. The dependent because he is convinced that he cannot do it by himself so consequently he links to another person he expects to take care of him the same way his parents did.

If we ask why parents are overprotecting their kids when it gives poor results, the answer to this question is in the minds of parents. Overprotecting parents love their children as other parents do, but they are obsessed with fear and concern to preserve their kid's life and health. These parents do not distinguish love from the concerns and worries.

Chapter 20: The Introverted Road To Success

How to be a Successful Introvert
According to the first wide-ranging research study of the Myers-Briggs Type Indicator (MBTI) in 1998, 50.7% of the population is more inclined to introversion. And in a more recent study, the introvert percentage even rose up to 57.

Now, you might find this quite confusing since your environment seems to be more extroverted. Or maybe introverts aren't just as noticeable as the extroverts, you guess. But, no. It's more likely that several of these introverts thought that putting off an extroverted façade will stop the endless misunderstanding. Perhaps they're thinking they'll succeed that way. But victory can't be conquered with that tactic. In fact, nobody has to fight introversion off.

To ensure a successful life, you must accept that your introverted side—no matter how small or big it may be—plays a dynamic role in your journey. From the previous chapters you have learned the real essence of introversion and the advantages it can give you. You have seen the lives of some people who succeeded, not "in spite of", but "as a result of" their introversion. Now, it's your turn to succeed in your own way. The following will be a set of advices on how to become a successful introvert.

Embrace being an Introvert

Before doing anything else, strip down all your misconception about introversion and swim into your true colors. If you find it hard, keep reminding yourself that you are not alone. Half of the population is just like you. You can go to social media and find like-minded people as you. Many social media platforms are available out there.

Chatting with people similar to you will help you appreciate introversion more. The idea of talking to 20 people in a day might sound exhausting but with social media have made it easy for you. You don't even have to leave your room.

You can also inspire yourself with people who have already succeeded (like those mentioned in Chapter 3). Follow their steps and focus on how they kept being themselves without being thrown off by the extroverted world.

Find your Passion

Look for something you are passionate about. Do you love painting? Teaching? Writing? Music? Discover what activity makes you feel alive. Let yourself get carried away by your limitless imagination and strive to be excellent in the career you chose. Your passion will serve as the burning fire that will drive you to achieve your goals.

If Bill Gates didn't have his extraordinary passion for computers, Microsoft wouldn't exist. Maybe he thought it's something the world needs, and you should ask yourself that same question. What do you think the world needs? What breaks your heart? Can you do something to help? Are you interested enough to seek and pursue it?

Learn to be curious and follow wherever that curiosity may take you. Steve Job's curiosity led him to learn typography and develop design sensibility skills, and that paved the way for the birth of the iPhone.

Look for something that wouldn't just aid your financial needs, but something that you would want to do for the rest of your life even if you don't get paid to do it; that's your passion.

Know your Strength and Weaknesses

Distinguishing where you are strong at and where you still need improvement is important to create an alleviated life. You have to understand your abilities.

Start by writing down the things you can and can't do. Ask yourself how and why you perform good or bad in that area.

185

Next is to mirror your values; they will be your guidelines to approaching life. By identifying your values, you will know what things your strength or weakness to you could be, regardless of what it may infer to others. Examine if your actions align with your values, if they don't then reflect again. It would be better if you tell someone else about your values to force yourself to be accountable for your actions.

Don't be Afraid to Socialize

There's nothing wrong with socializing because it will give you a wider range of people you can share your insights. If you find it difficult to socialize, there are certain techniques that will help make it a bit easier for you. You can start by copy-pasting social skills of some extroverts you admire. This doesn't mean that you're going to fake it or what, you just need to get some ideas how to start.

Next is to have control over the conversations during parties or group discussions. Avoid close-ended questions that can only be answered with yes or no. Try opening open-ended questions like "why do you think ___?" or "how is it that ____?" If it comes to the point that your energy is getting low, invite them to a low-key place that may help you recharge (like a coffee shop, park, etc.). Learn how to make your worlds intersect and socializing won't be that much problem for you.

Have a Consistent Quiet Time

Spending time with solitude may be hard to do today, especially if you've gotten used with a noisy and stressful environment. What you can really ensure for an outset is to begin in small steps.

Try practicing solitude for five minutes a day. It doesn't have to be in a noiseless and human-less place at all. Five minutes of silence in your bedroom while everyone's still asleep is a good start. Or you can take a five-minute walk before you go to bed at night. Practice solitude as often as possible and you'll find yourself craving for more.

Find a Safe Haven

If most people have dream houses, introverts have dream rooms. Having your own room will help you reenergize whenever you need to. Find a vacant room in your house and personalize it. Start by making a draft. Consider to include in your plan the things that will help you reenergize such as a bookshelf, dark curtains, a lamp (depending what kind of illumination is comfortable with you), and a comfortable chair.

If you don't have a vacant room in your house, find a nearby place where you can be alone. It can be a secluded bench in your local park or a far corner in your office's parking lot, a garden, a cemetery (this is creepy, but it works for some people), etc. Having your own private space will enable you to meditate. Just like the introvert facilitator of a meditation circle, Doug Imbrogno said: "Meditation allows you to not get swept away by the flood of thoughts and emotions, to sit by the side of the river, to watch the raging torrent and not get swept down."

In spite of where you wander during the day, always be reminded to take your mind with you. It's your fundamental private space. If your mind remains to free flow twisted thoughts, even if you are in the quiet place, it won't work. Take note of the things that feels right and what feels wrong. Make room for your desires. Try to always find clarity. Make improvements as necessary; exercise being straightforward with yourself, and most importantly, live a life full of love.

Keep Journals

As you get used with being alone with your thoughts, more and more astonishing ideas will flood your mind. However, your mind is not like a computer hard drive, you just can't save everything that you like. It's important to keep journals by your side to record these enormous thoughts. Those can be something phenomenal someday.

If you're not a fan of pen and paper, you can download journal-writing applications on your smartphone. You can even make use of journals as a place for the unnecessary emotions that you find unhelpful in the process of your growth.

You should record important reflections because you will not get that many reminders about the things you learned the day before. Journals will allow you to revisit previous learning and enable you to assess what has been your progress up to the present.

Think Outside the Box

Thinking outside the box sometimes means a little bit of craziness. Thinking outside the box requires creativity. And creativity empowers you to take the leverage of improvement higher. The more you move closer to improvements, the more likely you are going to succeed. From time to time, you need a changing perspective for you to see a problem or situation from different angles.

Some scientists, artists, architects, designers and others have the habit of observing and analyzing the nature to get inspirations. This has been a definitely fantastic strategy for people who want to think outside the box. By stepping into another world or another role, you will get many ideas that will aid at finding solutions to your problems. By being creative, you have the capabilities to offer something new to the progress of the world and the rest of humanity.

Take the Lead

During the Global Leadership Summit 2014, Carly Fiorina said that everyone has the potential to lead. Global Leadership Summit or GLS anyway is a gathering of different kinds of leaders across the globe.

In that particular summit, Susan Cain was also one of the speakers. In her speech, she talked about the value of allowing your team to think in both introverted and extroverted ways. She said that you should allow people to have a few moments of silence to be alone with their thoughts before making group discussion. If there's a leader who understood the power of introversion so much, it's Susan Cain. Susan Cain is an introvert herself. She, in fact, wrote the book, "Quiet: The Power of Introverts in a World that Won't Stop Talking."

Leadership is not merely about bossing around flocks of people, but simply believing in what you can do. It's making people follow you by displaying how you love your life and yourself. If they witness the greatness of the path you're choosing, they'll follow your lead.

Conclusion

I hope this book was able to help you to further understand what being an introvert means and how you can achieve the same, or even greater, levels of success as any naturally born extrovert.

The next step is to implement the tips and habits presented in this book. The contents of this book are meant to help you first accept who you are, and then subsequently improve your confidence so that you can conquer your anxiety and fears all the while showing the world who you really are and what you are capable of doing.

www.ingramcontent.com/pod-product-compliance
Lightning Source LLC
Chambersburg PA
CBHW071533030426
R18080100001B/R180801PG42336CBX00001B/1